THE EYES OF THE LION

CINDY YEE KONG

abbott press®

A DIVISION OF WRITER'S DIGEST

Abbott Press books may be ordered through booksellers or by contacting:

Abbott Press
1663 Liberty Drive
Bloomington, IN 47403
www.abbottpress.com
Phone: 1-866-697-5310

Because of the dynamic nature of the Internet, any web addresses or
links contained in this book may have changed since publication and
may no longer be valid. The views expressed in this work are solely those
of the author and do not necessarily reflect the views of the publisher,
and the publisher hereby disclaims any responsibility for them.

Any people depicted in stock imagery provided by Thinkstock are
models, and such images are being used for illustrative purposes only.
Certain stock imagery © Thinkstock.

ISBN: 978-1-4582-1239-9 (sc)
ISBN: 978-1-4582-1240-5 (e)

Library of Congress Control Number: 2013919867

Printed in the United States of America.

Abbott Press rev. date: 11/07/2013

Mrs. Kong's memoir is a blessing to believers and while my heart broke for her I could not stop reading at how Jesus turned her life around. If you are like me and enjoy a touching memoir, please read The Eyes of the Lion. Eva Shaw, Ph.D., ghostwriter and author, www.evashaw.com

If there is one word to help identify this writer, it's resilience. She never gave up even though she faced multitudes of physical and mental problems during her lifetime. Rising above these adversities, this writer's experiences and challenges give readers a better understanding of others who may not have had the positive experiences as they have had.

As an educator of more than 40 years in all levels of public education, I highly recommend The Eyes of the Lion for all educators in special education and cultural studies, both in K-12 and college education classes. This writer's personal life and decisions will enlighten readers and provide them with valuable insights as they work with their special needs students of all ages.

Dr. John N. Hatfield, Ph.D. (The University of Oklahoma, Adult and Community Education)

Acknowledgment

I would like to give special thanks to Dr. John Hatfield, Eve Ash, Eva Shaw, Karen Winfrey and Alicia Chesser for helping to make this memoir possible. Also, thanks to my special friend Mary Anne Walker for encouraging me not to give up on finishing this book, when things were caving in on me.

Nothing in the world can take the place of Persistence. Talent will not; nothing is more common than unsuccessful men with talent. ... Genius will not; unrewarded genius is almost a proverb. Education will not; the world is full of educated derelicts. Persistence and Determination alone are omnipotent. The slogan "Press On", has solved and will always solve the problems of the human race.

Calvin Coolidge, 30th president of the United States

Author's note

This memoir was draw from my personal experiences growing up in an alcoholic family. Names have been changed to protect the privacy of the individuals. In a few instances, time has been compressed and events rearranged for the purpose of story and narrative.

Does Anyone Care?

The Yorkville community is located on the Upper East Side of Manhattan. Someone once told me in the 1990s that to live in this community, you would have to be a lawyer or doctor of some sort. That might be the case in that era but it was not always so. My mom and I immigrated from Hong Kong to be reunited with the rest of our family, my two older brothers and my father, in 1980. I was only ten years old then. We lived on the third floor of a six-story red brick building on East 75th Street. Each floor had five apartments: two in front, two at the end, and one in the middle. The last floor was the rooftop where you could go and see things from above: the adjacent buildings' rooftops, the fire escape of each floor.

Each floor overlooked a patch of concrete that led to our neighbor's building. Clotheslines on each floor of our building connected our windows to theirs. When Mom had to wash big items, like bedspreads and blankets' covering, she hung them on a clothesline and wheeled it out into the open space to dry.

We lived in a two-bedroom apartment. My parents' room was in the hallway near the entrance door. Beyond the hallway, we had a tiny kitchen and bathroom in one, with a bathtub, a toilet with three walls and a door (thank goodness), and a small sink beside the tub in front of the wall of the toilet. The stove was in front of the sink and the tub, about four feet away from my room.

I shared my room with my two older brothers. It had one window looking out the back of the building, opposite the door. My oldest brother's wooden frame bed sat against the wall of our neighbor's apartment, in front of the window. My older brother slept in a metal frame bunk bed placed in front of my rollaway bed, which was right behind the wall of the bathtub.

My mom worked long hours in a sweatshop in Chinatown doing piece work; sewing pieces of cloth together to make a whole outfit. The whole outfit was worth ten cents or less. Occasionally she might get fifteen cents per outfit, and when she did she would stay busy working seven days a week and twelve hours or more a day. Her factory had rows of sewing machines with seamstresses sitting in front of them on metal chairs with no back support. Stacks of fabrics lay in front of the fire escape windows.

My mother had short curly black hair. She wore dark floral sheer blouses with white undershirts underneath and nylon pants. The only time I got to see her was when I got up early in the morning for school. She combed my hair and put it in two ponytails. She made congee rice for breakfast and we ate it with shredded pork.

"Mom, I am having a hard time in school and the kids are mean to me. I don't like science and I don't understand it."

"Go on, finish your breakfast and get downstairs to wait for your school bus."

"Mom," I begged in a loud whisper.

"Go on now."

I desperately wanted her empathy with my struggles. Why couldn't she give me five minutes of her time?

Dejectedly I went downstairs and sat at the end of the last stairway to wait for my school bus. December was a cold month. We got an inch of snow on Christmas Eve, and the temperature dropped from the thirties in the morning to under twenty by midnight. With my coat all zipped up, my scarf wrapped around my neck, and gloves on my hands, I could still feel the chill sweep over my body and face. I stood shivering.

A mini school bus parked in front of the building and a matron came out to get me. I headed out to her as soon as she stepped outside of the bus. "Good morning, Yee, how is it going?" she asked.

"Good morning." I headed to my seat.

The matron checked to make sure that I got my seat belt on. I was the first kid to get on the bus so I had to sit through the rest of the trip while they picked up the other students on their list. It was a tedious, long ride from home to school. I wished they didn't have to make all the other stops before they took me where I needed to be. When my stop came, the bus driver opened the door for the matron to get out first, then let me out, and the matron walked me to my classroom on the second floor.

My fourth grade teacher Ms. Silverman gave me a big smile as I stood in the doorway. "Good morning Yee, it is nice to see you. Please take your seat." She had curly red hair with thick bangs in the front and blue eyes.

"Hi, Ms. Silverman," I said shakily as I stumbled to my seat.

"Look at her, she walks funny and talks funny." One of my classmates, George, uttered these words, and the rest of them followed.

3

"AH HA HA HA!"

I didn't know the reason for my uncoordinated hands and feet. I had better control of them in the morning, having just woken up from a restful sleep. It progressively got worse as the day went on. I felt like bursting out in tears but couldn't, because I was simply trying to make it through the day.

Victor smiled at me with his darling little face. "Chin chow chin chow chin chain, ha ha ha."

"Victor, stop making fun of her. Leave her alone," Diana yapped at him. Diana was the only girl in my class that was nice to me. She had shoulder-length, thick brown hair and she chattered when she talked.

"Did you see the scene where the Woody Woodpecker got enormous strength from this stolen tonic bottle?" Miguel asked.

"Did you hear about what happened to Daniel's mom?" another added.

"I love the scene where Woody beats the bat and returns the stolen bottle," Alex said as he tried to mimic Woody's laugh before George smacked him on the head.

"Quit making a fool out of yourself, Alex."

The teacher didn't give us any assignments until about an hour later. The students spent that free time in an endless jabber. "Please get in a straight line outside the front door. It is time for lunch," Mrs. Silverman directed us.

We stood single-file in the hallway and followed our teacher to the cafeteria. Alex reached out his hand and yanked Diana's hair.

"Eeeyouch!"

The cafeteria was filled with students from different elementary grade levels. We had beef patties for lunch that day, with a small carton of milk and some peaches that came from a can. The line was long and I was tired of standing, so I squatted until I was served. Victor, who stood a few people ahead of me, turned around and looked at me with a smile.

"Why are you mean to me, Victor?"

"Ooh, chin chow chin chow. Ha, ha, ha."

He was a cute and adorable little boy, and whether he understood my uncontrollable words didn't really matter. I was hurt by the way he made fun of me. I was too crippled for anyone to like me.

I got my lunch tray and sat with my class group table. "*Hola*, Diana, *que pasa?*" A student hollered from the line.

"Hey, Maria!"

Victor put his hands on the table and started to beat it to make a nice rhythmic noise. I tried to ape his drum beat to feel included, but my attempt was ignored.

After I finished my lunch, I always went back to my classroom while the other students went outside to play. Diana often came to our classroom to see if there was something I wanted her to get for me at the food truck. I'd give her a dollar to get me a small bag of Funyons, or sometimes a knish. I sat there by myself until lunch period was over.

At the end of the school day, my matron came to my classroom to take me home. The bus dropped me off at the curb in front of my building from Public School 97 on the Lower East Side. The matron ensured that I got to my building safely by assisting me to the front door. I walked while my arms and hands, legs and feet twitched and shook uncontrollably. Slowly I walked up two flights of stairs clawing the handrail or climbing on hands and feet to push myself up the stairs. I opened the door of my apartment with my home key. My father sat in his usual seat, sipping his beer. The smell of Budweiser permeated the place as I walked past him to my room.

My father sat at the kitchen table that was placed against the wall of his room. His special seat had always been at the end of the hallway, at the end of the table. His hair was short, salt-and-pepper color, and he was skinny, with a wrinkled face.

The minute he woke up in the morning, he reached for his Budweiser beer. He popped the can open with his thumb and index finger and poured the beer into a glass cup. He sat there all day in the same clothes he woke up in--sweatpants and a yellow-stained, white-collared shirt--sipping on his drink and puffing on his cigarette with a sourpuss face.

"*Sa nu nai*! You mother fucker! Good-for-nothing bitch. All you ever do is just walk to your room…. Huh," he said, as he slammed his drink against the table.

I immediately threw my hand against the doorknob and swung the door closed. "What do you want from me?" I hollered back with my slurred speech.

My older brother Forrest stared at me with a mean streak from his bunk bed, shook his head and let out his breath. I stared back at him with my eyebrows furrowed, wanting his empathy so badly.

Forrest got out of his bed in his briefs and put on his jeans. He went to the kitchen and started making a meal for me and himself before work. He picked up the wok lying on top of the stove and carried it to the sink to fill it with water. He brought the wok back to the stove and boiled the water. When the water had boiled, he put in a chopped piece of pork ribs that he got from the refrigerator next to the stove and seasoned it with fish sauce. He let it simmer for about five minutes, then put in rice noodles and cooked it for another ten. He placed the rice noodle soup with pork ribs in two large ceramic bowls.

He sat in front of the table and I sat on the opposite end from my father.

"Brother, you know the kids in school were making fun of the way I talked. They said 'chin chow chin chow.'"

He opened the *World Journal* newspaper and started to read it, eating his noodle soup at the same time. I continued to try to get his attention.

"Brother, you know the kids in school were making fun of the way I talked. They said 'chin chow chin chow.'"

Still, he wouldn't say anything back to me but kept on reading his newspaper and eating his soup. Despondently I went back to eating my noodles. After Forrest finished his meal, he got ready to go to work. He put on his shirt and combed his hair in front of the mirror above the sink and brushed his teeth. After he was done, he headed for the door without any words of goodbye to me.

I went to my room to do my homework.

The Abuse

I n my room, next to my bed, I kneeled on the ground and pressed my toes against the floor to keep from frantic trembling and jerking so I could do my homework. I continually changed my position to put some kind of pressure on my toes to manage the spasms. My hands shook when I had to write but I couldn't press my hands against anything to stop the quiver like I did with my toes because I needed to use them. I took my time.

Reading was hard for me. I never knew why I had to read a sentence several times over before I fully processed what it said. I would read the first sentence and when I got to the second or the third sentence, I would forget what the first sentence was, so I would have go back to the first sentence and start over. I would have to read the sentence out loud several times to comprehend it. Sometimes I wouldn't get it regardless of how hard I tried, so I would memorize it to pass tests in college.

When I was done with my homework, I would go out in the semi-kitchen bathroom area to fill the tub with hot water so I could take a bath. One might wonder why we had a bathtub in an open space area. My father got the apartment in 1969--the year I was born- -and it was part of the architecture popular during that time. I remember seeing an episode of the show "The Honeymooners" where they showed a kitchen area with a bathtub in an open space. It was broadcast by CBS from 1951-1956 and was set in an apartment building in Bensonhurst, Brooklyn.

As soon as the water almost filled to the brim of the tub, I got my clean panties out and put them in a chair next to the tub.

"Dad, I am taking a bath. Go to your room."

"Ooh." He picked up his drink and headed to his room.

Within five minutes of immersing my body into the tub of hot water, my dad hollered from his room, "Are you done yet?"

"Not yet."

"Hurry up! You take too long."

I bathed quickly, then immediately dried my body with a face cloth and went into my room to put on my clothes.

"*Saya wor nuon*. I am done. You can come out," I said loudly.

After I put on my clothes, I came out to make dinner for myself. I got the pot from the rice cooker lying on top of a cabinet counter next to the stove. I arched my knees to the ground in between the refrigerator and the stove where the 25-pound bag of rice was, to scoop two cups of rice into the pot.

"You need to put one more cup of rice in," my dad demanded.

"But it is just fine the way it is," I answered.

Angrily he got out of his chair and came to where I was, swiped his hand across my head, and knocked me to the floor. I picked myself up, biting my lower lip in anguish, and stubbornly told him, "It is fine the way it is." I proceeded to the sink, washed the rice a couple times, and filled the pot with water to put it in the rice cooker.

Years later when I was in my early twenties, I was home from college on summer break, working as a cashier in my neighborhood drug store. As I was getting ready to go to work, my dad shouted from his usual chair, "You good for nothing mother fucker. You will never amount to anything. You are a horrible worker and you can't even keep a job more than a month. You are a worthless piece of shit."

In an irate tone of voice, I said, holding back my tears, "What about you? You think you are something. At least I am trying." He furiously smashed his glass cup against the table so that the beer splattered all over it and came after me. When I saw him coming, I lifted my feet up in the air to push him away. He hurried back to the kitchen, got himself a butcher knife, stood next to me and said, "Come on."

I withdrew from any further physical attempt. We stood there motionless for a few seconds with our evil eyes staring straight into each other.

He turned around to put the butcher knife away, sat in his seat, and lit up another cigarette. He inhaled and exhaled smoke out of his mouth. "Don't you dare mess with me, you bitch."

Mom was off from work on some weekends. On her days off she made a special effort to make me something I liked to eat. She would get up early in the morning to head to Chinatown for grocery shopping. She would take the number 6 train from 77th Street on Lexington Avenue to Canal Street.

The train pulled into the Canal Street station. She knew this was the stop she got off at, even though she couldn't read any alphabets nor any Chinese characters. She had her way of learning things. Since she could read numbers, she learned that it would be four stops after 14th Street to get to Canal, and she would count the stops attentively.

The street was filled with street vendors and displays of live fish in a tank or on top of crushed ice and vegetables outside the stores. In a crowd of people hurrying and minding their own business to do their chores in the busy streets of Chinatown, Mom walked around the Baxter Street area to find the best bargains.

"How much is the orange?" Mom asked.

"Ten for a dollar."

"Give me a dollar."

"How much this fish?"

"A dollar a pound."

"Yahhh, too much. Give me cheaper. Eighty cents, huh."

"*Chee sin ah*! You crazy! I need to make money."

She walked to another market and checked to see if they had something cheaper.

"How much fish?"

"Eighty cents."

"*Ho, ho*. Good. Give me this fish."

When Mom was done with her errand in Chinatown, she headed home to cook food for me. "Are you hungry yet?" she asked when she came home with bags of groceries.

"Yes, I am hungry. What are we having?" I asked with curiosity.

"I got you lobster and fresh noodles that you like. Hush, Dad is sleeping. I make you lobster noodle soup before he's up. Do you like?"

"Yes, Mom, I like it."

I waited with an ambivalent feeling, moving between excitement to eat my favorite food, seafood, and fear of my father. Will Mom get it all done before Dad gets up? Will I finish in time before he finds out about it? She lodged the lobster on a wooden cutting board and, with a butcher knife, she incised the bottom of the body and split it in half. Each half she cut into bite-size pieces. She boiled the water in the wok and placed the cut lobster into the boiling water. Then she put the fresh noodles into the wok. She used fish sauce for seasoning. At last, she got a large noodle bowl in the upper cabinet, put the soup in the bowl, and brought it to me.

"Now gobble up before he wake."

Heavy sigh. "All right."

I picked up the noodles with my chopsticks and expediently slurped them into my mouth, biting the lobster meat off the shell as fast as I could. Mom threw the shell of the lobster into the garbage can right after I was finished. I heard Dad clearing his throat from his room.

Petrified with fear, I trembled at the sound of his voice. What if he finds out? I wondered.

He came out of his room and sat in his usual seat, with beer can popped open and cigarette lit up. I hurried to my room. Mom started cleaning the apartment: the sink, floor, toilet bowl, kitchen stove. She got a mop out of the toilet room and a bucket from under the sink, filled the bucket with water and put laundry detergent in the water. She opened the door of my room and started mopping the floor. The first time she mopped with the laundry detergent, the second with plain tap water. When she was done, the apartment didn't look too bad to live in. Mom sure knows how to make a filthy apartment sparkling clean, I thought.

"You want cauliflower for dinner?" Mom inquired of me as I walked out of my room and sat on the kitchen table.

"You are spoiling her," Dad hastily responded.

"I just ask her."

"You spoil her. You raise her to be no good."

"Only one daughter. No wrong giving her cauliflower." Tears swelling inside her eyes.

Mom went to the refrigerator and got out a cauliflower. "Did you not hear me? You fucking bitch! You spoil her." Dad threw his beer can across the room, where it smashed the top part of the toilet door and shattered it to pieces.

I sat on the kitchen table bawling. "Why you crying? This is between me and your Dad."

I tried to contain myself from losing it and went to my room. *Why doesn't Dad like me? Why he is such a jerk to me? Does he not care about his family?* Sometimes I wished Mom were home, other times I wished she wasn't, simply because of the clashes they got into.

Usually I was home alone with Dad, battling to bathe myself, wash my clothes with my bare hands, make dinner for myself to eat, and get ready for bed for school tomorrow. My oldest brother and my mother usually came home from work after I was in bed.

My Brothers

ddle was the same age as me. His father was a distant relative, and my brother Forrest was very fond of him. Iddle was only about eleven years old when he first came to America. He was a rangy boy with flimsy straight hair and a squeaky tone of voice. My brother instantly connected with him on their first meeting and became a pal and a big brother to him even though there was a big age gap. He would take him out for a ride in his new car or to different outings. I wondered if my brother would like me better if I was a boy and physically able. Iddle and my brother sat at the dinner table, reminiscing about their trip that day.

"I like your new car. It rides smooth," Iddle commented.

"Ah yeah yeah, I like it too. That car is something. Isn't it?"

"You know that girl, in the Chinese restaurant we went to eat at, was eyeing you. I think she likes you."

"Teehee, hee, hee, hee," Forrest gave a bashful smirk.

"Let's do something today, but what? Any idea?"

"How about we go to Central Park?"

"Brother, I want to go, too," I interjected.

Sigh!

"Why not? I want to go too." I was tired of being cooped up in this apartment and had nowhere to go and no one who wanted to take me places. I was desperately pleading with my brother. It reminded me of a similar situation earlier in my childhood years in Hong Kong, before I became disabled.

My brother was going to the zoo with his friends, and he decided to take my landlady's son along, who was a year or so older than me.

"I want to go to the zoo, too."

"You can't go."

"Why can't I go? I want to go."

Sigh. He shook his head.

"Why not? I WANT TO GO."

"Let her go along," my mother insisted.

He immediately grabbed my landlady's son's hand and headed to the door quickly. I ran toward him and screamed after him. "I want to go. Why can't I go? Why won't he take me to the zoo?" My mother stood there in silence, watching me cry my eyes out.

Tears started swelling in my eyes when I heard the same answer repeated back to me, all these years later. "I want to go to Central Park, too. I have never been there."

Sigh. Then he gave a slight nod.

I was happy that my brother finally let me tag along. However, he and Iddle went ahead of me while I lagged behind with my arduous walking. I walked less than a quarter of a block before I had to take a break to catch my breath and rest my body before resuming. Occasionally they would stop to see if I was still in view. We headed west on 75th Street.

Why can't they slow down and wait for me? They are so far ahead of me. Why can't my brother carry me? Finally, they

15

got to Five Avenues, and then aimed for Conservatory Water, where they stopped and sat on the border benches while I caught up with them.

It was a beautiful sunny afternoon with the high beams of the sun's rays beating down on us, making us sweat. The gigantic pond called Conservatory Water was one of Central Park's main attractions that ran from 73th through 75th Streets. Rows of trees surrounded the pond. Iddle and Forrest sat along its bordering benches to appreciate the sight of a tiny model sailboat crossing its poised surface.

"Let's rent a boat," Forrest suggested.

"*Ho, ho.* Good," Iddle said, with a big smile on his face.

They went east of the pond to Kerbs Memorial Boathouse to rent a boat. "One boat," my brother said to the cashier behind the counter. The cashier rung the cost on her register, then directed them where to go for the boat.

I sat on the bench waiting while my brother paddled the boat on the shimmering water, enjoying the smell of crisp clean fresh air and water, the sound of birds chirping, the surrounding nature and its company. Around the border of the pond, bird-watchers crowded the area with their binoculars in hand, watching for signs of the famed red-tailed hawks of Fifth Avenue.

To the west of the Conservatory Water were the vibrant spring colors of white and pink blooming cherry trees. On the northern side, a sculpture of Alice in Wonderland, from Lewis Carroll's 1865 fantasy classic, larger than human size, caught the attention of visitors.

They pulled in their tiny model sailboat from the pond. "Let's take a picture with the statue," Iddle remarked.

Forrest nodded without words.

Forrest sat on the lap of Alice and next to her kitten Dinah. He smiled, and Iddle snapped.

"There is another statue. Let's take a picture on that," Iddle suggested.

Forrest nodded his head again in agreement.

"Excuse me, take a picture please?" Forrest inquired of a passerby.

"Sure."

We all gathered around and sat on a different part of the sculpture. My brother sat on the lap of Hans Christian Andersen, with his fingers squeezing the sculpture's nose and his other hand pressed against The Ugly Duckling book that shared Andersen's lap. Iddle ascended to the top of the author's head, and I stood on the bench that Andersen perched on and placed my two fingers in "devil horn" formation behind Iddle's head.

"Smile." The stranger snapped the shutter.

I wished I was a boy, not a girl. I just wanted my brother to like me. I endeavored to act like a tomboy to gain his acceptance and his attention, so later, back in the apartment, I boldly placed my feet up on the dinner table.

"Put your feet down," my mother snapped at me.

"Why do I have to? Forrest can do whatever he wants. Why can't I do the same?"

"I told you to put your feet down or you'll fall over."

"But I don't want to."

Every attempt I tried was to no avail. Forrest still didn't pay attention to me.

Then there was my oldest brother, Bo, who at one time I had to ask for a few bucks to get some school supplies.

"Big brother, can I get some money?"

"What do you need the money for?" he catechized me suspiciously.

"I need to get some pens. It is only a couple of dollars."

"Why do you need it?"

"For school!"

Gosh, it was only a couple of dollars. What kind of evil could I do with it? Why was he being so suspicious of me, like I was going use that money to do drugs or something! He wouldn't say anything as to whether he would give me the money or not.

"Mu mu. Little sist. Let go."

He took me to 75th Street and First Avenue, to the Rainbow Pharmacy. "Give me a pen," he asked a cashier behind the counter. The cashier got a pen from behind her register, rang it up, and my brother paid for it. He gave the pen to me.

I headed home and he went to work. That was the first and the last time I ever asked him for money.

My Life Before Disease

Because I left China at the early age of five, finding my heritage has been a challenge. Where I was from and what my life was like before I got my disease is not easy to reconstruct. I have vague memories of the house I was born in. Otherwise, all the information I have was learned online or given to me by someone who grew up in China.

I know I come from Dong Qi Cun, Fuzhou, Fujian, China. But I didn't know anything about these places until a friend helped me understand. He explained to me that Fujian was a province, like a state; Fuzhou was the capital city of Fujian; and Dong Qi Cun was a village within the city of Fuzhou. Dong Qi Cun was where I was born.

Fujian was a province with many cities, among them Fuzhou, Jinjiang, Quanzhou, Xiamen, and Zhangzhou . (I know, I have a hard time pronouncing them myself, too.) Fujian has a current population of approximately 38 million with only 2 million in Fuzhou. China as a whole has more than 1 million population.

My friend also told me Fuzhou (also known as Foochow) was near the Pacific Ocean. People in earlier times living in that region knew about the other parts of the world, like

America. The first generation of Chinese in America came from that area as well as from Canton, which was also located in the Pacific Ocean.

I remembered 1975, when I was only five years old, sitting on the kitchen "hard bed," which was a raised wooden platform with straw attached to each top corner, watching my mother using the grindstone to crush some herbs into small pieces.

An avalanche of raindrops pounded on the the rooftop, followed by sporadic crashing thunder. I was tremendously frightened by it, my body jumping at every sound. I clutched close to Mom for comfort and safety at every opportunity I got.

Suddenly a scream tore through the air. Mom went out to see what happened, but I wouldn't let her leave my sight, so she carried me in her arms to go outside of the house.

"What happened?" Mom asked a woman who was crying heavily.

"He has been struck by lightning!" The woman stooped on her knees next to her husband's body, which lay lifeless on the concrete ground. She pounded her fist against her chest and sobbed uncontrollably. "I told you not to leave the house!"

"What happened?" The neighbors opened their front wooden doors to see what was causing the commotion. When they saw the unfortunate accident, they stood in silence, and felt remorseful for this young widow. The whole crowd seemed to sigh in unison, expressing their sympathy for her late husband.

My other memory of my early childhood years in China was the day I was standing outside of my red brick house wearing my pants with an open seam in the back, getting ready to go to a portrait studio.

Young children in China wear open seam pants so they can conveniently squat and go whenever they need to without the help of an adult. Parents leave baby bottoms uncovered for early infant toilet training so when the babies have to pee or poop, the parents simply hold the baby over a toilet, an outdoor latrine or simply open ground until business is done.

"Yee, put on a clean pair of pants and a jacket," Ming, our neighbor across from our house, called out in a high-pitched tone. She went to the clothesline and unclipped some clean clothes. "You need to look nice for this portrait." Ming was looking after me while mom was at work.

"Why?"

"It is for your Daddy to see how you have grown."

"Where is Daddy? How come I don't see him?"

"He in America, making big money for you."

"Why can't he make money here?"

"No big money here. American money is gold!" She gave me plain cotton trousers and lightweight cotton jacket with buttons. I didn't own anything colorful. Back in those days, the People's Republic of China wanted us all to wear similar clothing. My hair was short, a little bit below my ears. Most women's hair was kept short, and if it was long, it was braided or in a ponytail. Being functional, comfortable and efficient was of higher priority than looking pretty.

I buttoned my jacket all the way with no shirt inside it and put on my trousers. The jacket was considered a regular shirt.

Ming took me to the portrait studio. There, a man stood behind a daguerreotype camera and had me stand before a setting of trees, flowers, and a bridge over a river.

He put a large plate into the back of the camera and had me stand there until enough exposure had occurred. He then held the flash in his hand and snapped it. The picture was taken, and the flash of the light illuminated the room.

The neighbor took me back home, where I found that Mom had received a letter from the State Council. Yat, one of the villagers, translated it for her: "You have been approved to go to Hong Kong." The only bad thing was that Bo's application wasn't approved yet. Bo filled out a separate application because he was older. It took three years of waiting for this to come through. Meanwhile, our news spread throughout the neighborhood.

"*Ya houl.* Very good. You go to Hong Kong. Me wishes leave here and go with you," Yat said as he stood next to the kitchen door.

My mother was overjoyed with the news, but she restrained herself from displaying such emotion. It wasn't appropriate to show feelings of happiness or anything else during that era, for it would seem selfish. At the same time, she was sad that Bo wasn't approved yet. But she knew Bo was old enough to take care of himself. I secretly thought Mom would be happy to get out from under grandma's and aunt's maltreatment.

"Ha, you approve to go." My father's brother's wife, Chit, said in a snappy tone. She had short, straight hair of even length and famished facial features. Her husband passed away before I was born. They had three children. Her youngest boy was two years older than me. My father had been their financial supporter since her husband died. My mother stood in silence as she carried on about how my father didn't want her to go to Hong Kong.

"Well, Sim lived in Hong Kong for a period. Why can't his wife and kids follow his path? He has connections there for them," Yat answered my aunt back.

Mom went upstairs to our room and started to pack the few clothes that we had. We all got a good night's sleep the night before our trip. Mom, Forrest and I took a tricycle caddy, where we rode on a coach behind the tricycle rider, all the way to the bus station. Mom bought three bus tickets to Foochow. When the bus came in with passengers waiting to get out, nobody gave each other space and time to let the people off the bus. They just headed for the entrance as the inside passengers were pushing their way out. Some of them even climbed through the windows.

My mother carried me in her arms and my brother Forrest, who was about thirteen or fourteen at the time, walked by her side as we pushed through the crowd and quickly claimed the available seats. It was a hot, sweaty summer, and people had to sit in close quarters. You could smell their stinky breath and feel their sweat as they pressed against you.

Once we got to the city of Foochow, we took a train to Guangdong Province to the city of Shenzhen, immediately north of Hong Kong. It was a tiresome, all-day trip. We left early in the morning from our village, and we didn't get to Shenzhen until late at night.

We took another train from Shenzhen to Lo Wu. Lo Wu or Lowu is an area in North District, New Territories, Hong Kong. Lo Wu lay between Hong Kong and mainland China and served as an immigration checkpoint for people crossing between mainland China and Hong Kong.

We stood in the customs line, waiting for them to stamp us to go through Hong Kong. My mother gave the man our authorization letter and he looked at it, nodded his head, and stamped for us to pass through.

Ling waved her hands frantically at us in the crowd as soon as she saw us pass through security. Ling was a friend of the family and our connection in Hong Kong. My mother saw her and led us to where she was standing.

"*Hay, hay, hay.* Here, here, here," Ling shouted from afar.

"*Hay.* Here. This is Aunty Ling." Mom introduced us.

"You tired. Long trip, huh. Let's go."

She helped us to find a place to live. We rented a room with a lady who had two boys and a daughter. We had a metal bunk bed where Mom and I slept on the bottom, and Forrest slept on top.

Hong Kong was composed of Hong Kong Island, Kowloon Peninsula or Kowloon, and New Territories. There are a total of eighteen districts in those three territories. We lived in Kowloon. In the early days, Catholic missionaries were evangelizing China but were painfully persecuted by the Chinese. They later fled to Hong Kong, where they were able to build Catholic schools and hospitals. Hong Kong was a British colony from 1841-1997.

I went to a Catholic kindergarten, where I had nuns as my teachers. As early as elementary school, the kids got a grade from 0-100. If a student did not have a passing grade, his or her scores would be written in red ink. You got tests every two months. Then they added up your score, calculated your average, and ranked you based on your scores out of the total students in the class. The student with the highest grade out of the whole class would get a rank of 1; the student with the lowest grade would be a rank 45, which represented the total number of students and the bottom of the class. Those who were ranked 1-10 were considered top of the class. I was ranked 3rd or 5th out of the whole class.

One day in class, a student threw a paper across the room to another student and then back at me.

"Stop it. The teacher won't like it and we need to be good," I whispered under my breath while the teacher had her back turned.

They continued throwing the paper back and forth, but this time I picked it up and threw it back at them. The teacher just happened to turn around and saw me throwing a piece of paper across the room.

Oh, I was so busted, and yet I didn't instigate it!

"Yee, you are the top student in the class and you need to set an example for the others to follow, therefore I must punish you."

"But--"

"I don't want to hear your 'but'."

The nun got a ruler out and smacked my hand with it. That was a corporal punishment for anyone who misbehaved and got caught. The key word was getting caught.

During recess, I played "red light green light," "one two three," and "rock, paper, scissors" with a group of girls. The boys played ping-pong and soccer.

Learning and getting good grades was effortless for me. I remembered every lesson given by the teachers without having to take notes or study hard. All I had to do was to pay attention in class. Things started to shift, however, during my third grade year.

One day I was walking down the street with my mother when, all of the sudden, I fell to the ground for no apparent reason. Over the next few days and weeks, my hands got weaker; soon I couldn't hold on to the papers I helped my teacher pass back to the students. Little by little, I began having problems with walking and my hands and feet began to tremble.

"I don't know what's wrong with her," Mom told Aunty Ling.

"How she gets this way?"

"It happened unexpectedly."

"Tomorrow, I take her to a doctor in a public hospital."

Aunty Ling took me to see a doctor the next day as she had promised. The doctor examined my eyes with his flashlight, looked through my ears with an otoscope, and checked my reflexes by hitting my knees with a reflex hammer.

"Has she gone through any traumatic events recently ?" The doctor asked.

"No, she was just a normal little kid."

"I can't tell what's wrong with her until she gets further testing. Are you the mother?"

"No. I am a friend of the family."

"The parents need to be here to authorize the tests."

Aunty Ling took me home and explained to my Mom what the doctor said. Mom called Dad in America to explain to him about what happened to me.

"Your daughter is having problems with her legs and hands," Mom told Dad.

"What wrong with her?"

"She can't walk. I need some money to take her to China to see doctors, to get her better."

"I need to call Chit to have her to come over and see it for me."

My Aunt Chit also was approved to go to Hong Kong with her children after we left. Dad arranged for Aunt Chit to come over to see if I was really having a problem.

"Yee, walk for me," Aunt Chit said.

I walked a little, then my hands and feet would get out of control and tremble. "*Iyol*! Oh my! What's wrong with her walking?"

"I don't know. It just happened all of a sudden," Mom answered.

Aunt Chit confirmed with Dad that I was really having a problem, so he sent money to Mom to take me back to China to see doctors.

Life Before Disease Part 2

Mom took me out of school during the second quarter to take me back to China while Forrest remained in Hong Kong. As usual we took the train from Shenzhen to Foochow and from there we took a bus to the rural area and waited at the bus station for an available tricycle caddy to take us to Dong Qi Cun, our village. A man rode up in his caddy and stopped in front of us.

"Where to?" he asked.

"Dong Qi Cun," Mom told him.

"Hop in, I'll take you to it."

I felt the breeze of the air blowing on my face as he accelerated. We passed through different villages with a sight of pedestrians walking aimlessly, flapping their fans to ward off the heat, while others were in a hurry to do their errands. We were as much a spectacle to them as they were to us.

Finally the tricycle driver drove us up to the side of the house. Grandma heard us from the road. She did not come out to greet us nor help us with the luggage. Mom carried a small suitcase into the house and came right back out while I remained seated in the coach. She paid the man and carried me inside.

"Mother-in-law," Mom greeted Grandma, and directed me to do so as well.

"Grandma," I said.

Grandma nodded her head and gave us a faint smile. "Are you hungry? There is cook noodle in the kitchen."

"No, no, no, you eat that noodle. We make something for ourselves," Mom responded.

News got around quickly that we were home because of my walking difficulty. Ming and Yat came over to visit us.

"What happened to her?" Yat asked Mom.

"I don't know."

"Oh my, her hands and feet are trembling uncontrollably," Ming remarked.

"There is a Chinese medicine doctor that I know. He is in Foochow City. I'll bring you to him."

"I was thinking of taking her to our relative, who practices Western medicine, but I'll go to see that doctor as well. Whatever helps!"

Mom carried me on her back to see both Eastern and Western doctors in the city of Foochow on many hot summery days, as often as I needed.

Mom also sought out an answer in the Buddhist temple. She took me there to burn incense to the idols and search for an answer in the Chinese fortune stick. The Chinese fortune stick was a long cylindrical bamboo cup or tube with a hundred flat sticks inside.

She kneeled in front of the statues and shook the cylinder, with the flat sticks tipped slightly downward, until at least one stick left the cylinder and dropped onto the floor. Whatever one dropped to the floor was the answer to what she was seeking.

The flat stick had a number, which needed to be translated by a monk. Mom gave the number to a monk and he pulled out an oracle that matched the number on the flat stick.

"Your ancestors are not happy. The great-grandma pushed your daughter down to the ground while she was walking. You need to burn more gold paper money and food offerings to them," the monk told her.

"*Iyo*! Oh no! I need to worship them more often so they leave my daughter alone."

Mom hurried home to prepare food for the food offering and bought gold paper money for a burnt offering. She cooked a whole chicken in boiling hot water, placed it on a plate, and laid it on the table with the rest of the food.

Grandpa's and Great-grandma's pictures were on the wall against the table. Mom lit the incense with a match and bowed three times, holding the incense stick in the palm of her hand. "Oh, our ancestors, protect Yee from sickness," she prayed, and placed it in an incense holder. Then she burned gold paper money in the tin garbage can, so they could use it in their afterlife.

When the ancestral worship ended, Ming's daughter, Jing Jing, came into the house with a Dalmatian puppy "Do you want this puppy?" she asked. "The mother just gave birth to her and the family are giving the puppies away because they're too many mouths to feed."

"I sure would like to. Mom, can I?" I asked.

"You could have it for the time you are here," Mom said. "Once we leave, we can't bring it with us."

"Can I hold him, Jing Jing?"

Jing Jing transferred the puppy into my arms.

"Ohhhh! He is so cute."

The puppy followed me everywhere I went, with its tail wagging incessantly. It helped to fill the empty space of my life and kept me from boredom. "Oh come on, puppy, follow me to the pig barn. You want to race me there."

"Arf, arf, arf."

The puppy jumped up and down and wagged its tail. We raced against each other to the pig barn. "Oh, puppy that was fun. You must be hungry by now. Come on, let's go home so I can feed you rice."

Going back and forth, being treated by two different kinds of doctors, taking shots and bunches of herbs daily, I eventually got better. However, no one could tell us the cause. "Time to return to Hong Kong now you better," Mom uttered.

I wasn't ready to go, especially when I knew I would have to leave my puppy behind, and I was enjoying the freedom of not having to go to school. The next morning dawned, Mom and I got ready to go to the bus station. We walked to the main road of the village and waved for a tricycle caddy. The caddy came and we hopped in.

The puppy followed me through the main road and chased after us when the tricycle caddy carried us to the bus station. It kept running until the tricycle outran it. He was sad to see me departing and his face became droopy. I could hear him whining pitifully.

"Go home puppy, you can't come with us," I explained.

Its cries echoed in my ears as I rode further into the distance. I wished I could explain to him so that he could understand. Mom comforted me by telling me a story about someone who had left his dog behind because his job shifted him to a different country, but when he returned, the dog came back as well, wagging its tail and waiting for him. I felt hopeful and wished that my dog would come back looking for me when I returned once again.

I was exhausted by the time we got to our room in Hong Kong. Finally I was able to get a decent rest. After a day of rest, Mom took me to school. At first I had a difficult time speaking Cantonese since, in the past few months in China, I had spoken Foochow all the time. In no time, however, I was able to get back in the groove again.

My brother was making fun of me for having a difficult time speaking Cantonese. "Now you are a country girl," he said when I got home from school.

"I am not. I am a city girl," I retorted.

The following day of school, the teacher announced to the class that we were going to have a final next week.

Oh no, I just got back and we are having a final!

There wasn't much time for me to prepare and study. The students wore uniforms —the boys, white collared shirts with cotton pants and dress shoes; the girls, the same shirts but with cotton pinafores. Soon we had all congregated nervously in a classroom to take final exams in all the different subjects that were taught. These tests would determine our fate, whether we would be promoted to fourth grade or not! Fortunately, I was able to remember what was taught to me before I got sick and was taken out of school, and passed with a rank of 20 out of the whole 45 students.

Coming to America

Mom was making stir-fried cauliflower with soy sauce, steamed pompano, and rib bones broth with daikon for dinner. "Forrest, set up the table to get ready for dinner," Mom instructed.

Forrest went to the kitchen to get the utensils out. He set the rice bowls, chopsticks, and small Chinese spoons on the plywood folding round table of our room. "Put the roast pork I bought on the plate, Forrest." Mom knew that roast pork and cauliflower were my favorite dishes, and she made every effort to get me some at every meal.

After all the dishes had been cooked, Forrest fetched the meal from the kitchen and laid it on the table. The savory fragrance of the cauliflower and the hot steamy fish permeated the atmosphere. My hunger was ready to be indulged by these luscious foods. We all gathered together at the dinner table to feast on the meal and watch the show on TV in the living room that the landlady had on. But Mom was distracted, and kept turning her head around to look at the clock.

"What time is it now?" She turned her head again. "Dad is going to call around 7 o'clock. It is now 6:30." We didn't talk about how our days were, like some families do, or have much of any dialogue during the meal. It wasn't a social event or a moment of pleasure, but something necessary for survival: eating to stay alive. We eventually finished our meal around seven.

Fifteen minutes past seven, the phone rang. It startled me and interrupted the landlady's family's favorite soap opera. The landlady picked up the phone before Mom got to it. "Sue it is for you," she muttered.

Mom picked up the phone receiver. "Hay hay, how are things. Oh, you know the same old, same old. Yes, Forrest turns eighteen. You want him to go to America."

Mom didn't argue but just went along with Dad, since Forrest wasn't excelling academically. "Maybe he could earn a living there," she said. She tried to get him help with his school work by getting him into an after-school tutoring program, but he still wasn't very motivated to study.

Aunty Ling's husband got Mom hooked up with someone that earned a black-market income by helping people to get travel visas to go to America with large sums of money up front. It all happened so quickly that before I knew it, Forrest was gone.

Now it was just me and my Mom in the room. Mom took me to visit Aunty Ling often. Aunty Ling owned a co-op on her floor. She and her husband lived in this long, gigantic room that almost took up the whole floor. They had their own private bathroom, bedroom and living room. Behind her room, there was another door on the left side that opened to two adjoining rooms, rented by a family of tenants. In front of her private space there was a table with chairs for her guests and tenants to gather. On the rooftop, she had a metal structure about seven to eight feet in height, with no amenities, divided into two levels and rented by numerous male tenants who shared a sleeping area. All her tenants shared the same bathroom and kitchen on her floor.

I usually went to her private area to have some quiet time for myself so I could do what I wanted without anybody knowing. I chewed and swallowed the Double Mint gum that I was not supposed to, but it tasted better eating it than chewing alone.

Then I played with her nesting dolls, opening the largest size until I got to the smallest size, then closed them back in from the smallest to the largest, while Mom and Aunty Ling had some adult time.

In my moments of solitude, I thought about Dad. I wondered if I would ever see him. I closed my eyes, imagined Dad's picture in our room, and how joyful it would be to be carried in his arms, playing and patting his face, and leaning close to him for affection. I wondered when that day would come for me to be in my Dad's arms, now that both of my brothers were there with him.

"Ling, you don't know what kind of treatment I went through with Sim's family when he was in prison for eight years," Mom blurted out.

"You don't say."

"Chit spat on me and said the most hideous and derogatory words to me."

I came out of the room in the middle of Mom's conversation and asked her when we were heading home.

"In a minute, dear." She continued. "When things went missing in the house, she accused me of stealing them. She called me the wife of a criminal. Sim's mother stole food from me that I worked hard to put on the table to feed those two boys and gave it to Chit's household."

Sigh. She shook her head. "That was a hard time, but it is in the past."

"That was the hardest time, raising those two boys all by myself," Mom said, sharing the pain of her struggle.

"Now Forrest is gone, you can ask Sim to send you two as well. Maybe this way you can be a family together."

"Presently Sim is in buddy with her. Go figure."

I stood there looking from one to the other and listened to Mom's story. "They accused me of killing Sim's father when in fact he died of cancer." She took a deep breath to let out her tension. Ling patted Mom on the shoulder.

I had to wait a long time for Mom to finish telling her story before we got to go home.

After we left Aunty Ling's building, we always stopped by a tea shop and Mom bought me a cool refreshing Chinese Clear tea to drink. Drinking that tea on a hot summer day helped to cool off the sweat and quench the thirst.

I asked Mom when we were going to see Dad as we walked past a jewelry store on our way home. "I've never seen him. When are we going to America?"

"I don't know, Yee. I'll talk to your Dad next week about that."

Mom called Dad the following week from our apartment. "Did Forrest get there safe and sound?" she asked immediately.

"Yeah, he's right here." Dad gave the phone to Forrest.

"I got here ok, Mom." Forrest's voice sounded staticky.

"Yee, say hi to your Dad."

Mom handed the phone receiver to me. "Hi Dad! When are you coming over to see me?"

Dad was silent for a few seconds, then he said he needs money to come to see me and he can't go back to America once he leaves.

"Then I'll come over..."

Mom grabbed the phone from my hand and reminded Dad that I had never seen him since I was born. "She needs to see you."

"You know I can't leave here," Dad answered.

"Now that Forrest and Bo are there, it is time for the whole family to be there."

"All right, I will send you money and you can make the arrangements with Ling's husband," Dad responded.

Mom called Aunty Ling after she finished talking to Dad and told her the good news. "Sim is going to send the money for our trip to America," Mom said.

"That is good."

"I need Yong to make the necessary preparations for me."

Later we met Aunty Ling's husband at their home. Yong took us to the office of a man named Sung, who had helped Forrest to get his traveling visa. Before we headed out, he asked Mom if she had the money.

"Yes. It's in my purse."

"When you get there, pay attention to what they tell you, and follow their instructions on your trip." Mom nodded her head in agreement.

Mom and Sung met and they exchanged pleasantries. "This lady and her child need to go to America. Help them get there," Yong explained.

"You got the money?"

Mom handed him a brown paper bag with money inside.

"Now I can get started on the necessary paperwork to get your two traveling visas. You are going to fly to South America first; then you're gonna fly to America. I'm gonna be your inconspicuous tourist guide. I will be in the background along the trip to make sure you get through."

Sung filled out the application for our travel visas, and it was approved. We met again for him to give us the visas and airplane tickets. I was so excited that I was finally able to see Dad that I tossed and turned all night before our trip. On the morning of our trip, we had breakfast and headed to Kai Tak International Airport, which was notorious for the casualties that had occurred at its precariously-positioned landing strip, located right next to a residential area.

Coming to America Part 2

Mom stood on the edge of the curb of a busy intersection and waved her hand to signal a taxi. A taxi stopped and we quickly got into it. "Where to?" the driver asked.

"Kai Tak Airport," Mom replied.

"All right."

On the way to the airport we encountered a traffic jam. The cars barely moved an inch in the next ten minutes. The driver rolled down his window enough for him to tuck his head out and holler angrily, "Hurry up! What's the hold up?" He waved his fist in the air and honked his horn relentlessly.

Not until I had moved to the Midwest in the later part of my adult life, did I wonder why the drivers felt the need to impulsively honk their horns continuously in the city of New York and Hong Kong when they faced traffic jams, as if honking would help them to get out of the traffic jam quicker.

The taxi driver was finally able to maneuver and get out of the jam and brought us to the airport in a timely manner. He stopped at the airport's main entrance. Mom paid the taxi driver and carried our vinyl sport bag strapped to her shoulder. I clung tightly to her hand.

People scrambled in and out of the airport and hurried to their destinations like speeding bullets, while Mom walked slowly among them, running her eyes over the crowd in search of Sung. Unfortunately, our speed wasn't tracking with the crowd's, and we ended up bumping into someone. "*Iyol*! Watch where you going!" the passerby grumbled. Mom stooped her head low in an apologetic gesture.

Finally we saw Sung in the airport. We were careful not to show our acquaintance with him. Subtly, we went to where he was standing. Imperceptibly, Sung introduced us to two men that were on the same journey as we were. One was six feet tall, married with children whom he had to leave behind in search of "gold money" in America. The other man was in his early twenties, skinny and average in height. Sung was careful to instruct us to reconnect when we landed in South America. We followed Sung to the airline that we were supposed to fly with, then we scattered apart.

It was my first time flying and I didn't know what to expect. The airline personnel announced different groups of seats to be boarded at different times. When our group was announced, we boarded the plane and found our seats. I wondered if all the other passengers were going to the same place as we were.

It was an overnight flight that took more than 12 hours, with time zones changing as we crossed over the United States. Hong Kong was twelve hours ahead, so when we crossed over we went back in time. I was uncomfortable in the plane and barely slept from being in an upright position. The airplane food was unappetizing. Eventually the announcement came that we would be landing in the United States in the next hour.

I slid the window shade up to see the landing and escape from the high altitude for the first time. I saw the extra wings flap open, heard the roar of the engine soaring, then slowly descending from the midst of the cloud and gliding onto the concrete ground. As we came closer, the piece of land became a road, buildings and cars. It was a spectacular experience.

"Ladies and gentlemen, we have landed in the United States. It is now 12:00 pm. We hope you enjoyed your flight with us. Please be seated until the seatbelt sign is turned off," the steward announced on the loudspeaker.

We all stayed seated until we had the signal to unbuckle our seatbelts. We stood up and waited for people ahead of us to exit the airplane so we could get out. We asked the steward for help on our way out to our connecting flight.

For the first time in my life, as my feet stood flat on the airport ground, I saw a white Caucasian, or as the Cantonese call them, a "white ghost" hustling about. I kept staring at the white ghost as my mother pulled me along and wondered why they looked different from me or the people that I normally saw. Their hair, facial structure, pupil colors and body build were quite odd and interesting at the same time. I was perplexed by their difference. How come my hair wasn't blonde or reddish like theirs?

Sung snuck up behind us and helped us to get to the connecting flight. I held Mom's hand close in mine as I followed her. We waited in line as people ahead of us boarded the plane. When Mom and I finally got to the inside of an airplane and found our seats in the middle aisle, we saw a lady breastfeeding her baby on the right of me, without any obstruction. A man who sat near her kept staring at her breast with his head and glasses tilted down. I got the impression that white men were perverts.

We reconnected with Sung and the two other men when we landed in South America. When we walked to the front door of the airport, there were two ladies flirting with the other two men, who reciprocated their flirts and went with them. Later they met up with us at the hotel where we were staying.

I don't remember which country in South America I went to, but I was there for the next two weeks. We stayed in a run-down hotel with roaches crawling on the walls. Sung's older brother lived there. He had married a woman from that country and they had a boy a couple years younger than me, with whom I played to pass some idle time. His brother owned a Chinese restaurant, and we ate there every day.

Sung's brother helped us to make the connection to fly to the United States. When we got to the airport in New York, we waited in line at the checkpoint to give our tourist visas to the immigration official. The immigration official looked at our visas with suspicion. "What are you here for?" he asked.

Mom didn't understand what he was saying, so she stood there in silence and stared at him blankly. "You speak English. There is a problem with your visas. I can't let you through." He made a phone call to have someone to come over to attend to us. Although the other two men did not stand in the same line with us, they faced a similar problem.

Later, men in suits and ties showed up where we were waiting and transported us from the airport to a hotel. They put Mom and me in a separate room from the other two men, and they stayed up all night with coffee to keep an eagle-eye on us while playing a game of cards to kill time.

I was shocked and afraid of what could happen to us, and what they would do to us. I had thought the process of disembarking would be a cinch; unfortunately, it turned out to be more complicated than I had expected. Of course we didn't get any sleep with them hovering over us and the commotion of their social activity. I wondered if this was the end of the road and whether we would be barred from going to New York to be with our family.

On the following day, the men took us back to the airport and got us onto a flight to Hong Kong. As I sat in the airplane seat, I pondered how my hope and anticipation of seeing Dad was being shattered at this very moment. I began to cry profusely and told my Mom that I would never get to see him, and how privileged she was to have seen him.

The steward announced on the speaker in both English and Chinese that they were going to make a stop in Philadelphia to fill up on gas. I was elated to hear that and immediately realized that we would have another opportunity. "Mom, we can escape from Philadelphia." Mom looked at me and smiled at what she thought was a joke.

Soon after the airplane landed in Philadelphia, a steward escorted us to a man who wore thick black-framed glasses and had black curly hair. He was supposed to keep tabs on us, to make sure we didn't leave the airport and board the plane. We followed his lead until he got distracted talking to an airport employee and bent his head down low to fill out some paperwork.

We saw a chance to walk away without his noticing, so we did, and went gung-ho to the nearest exit. We walked as fast as we could until we saw ahead of us a door that opened to the outside of the airport. Sung snuck up behind us again. "Are you guys escaping?" he asked.

"Yes, we are," Mom replied as we hurried to the door.

"When you get out, tell the taxi to get you to a bus station." And he taught me how to say it in English.

We crossed through the open door and we kept walking until we found a taxi right alongside the curb.

"Where to?" the driver asked.

"Bus station," I responded.

"Which one?"

"Ahhh?"

He kept driving until we passed through a busy intersection where we saw numerous taxis, and we spotted one of cab drivers who appeared to be Chinese. We got out of the taxi we were in and tried to get into the other.

"You Chinese?" Mom queried him in Cantonese as we climbed inside.

"Yes."

"Can you drive us to New York?"

"I need permission from my boss to do that. You could take a plane over."

"My daughter gets sick flying. She throws up."

"Are you guys escaping?"

"Oh, heavens no!"

I think deep inside the cab driver knew we were escaping, even though Mom denied the allegation. It was dreary and drizzly weather, and he didn't want to drop us off anywhere without knowing that we were safe and could reach our destination.

"Why don't I take you home to get dry. Then I could call my boss and get permission to drive you to New York," he suggested.

"Oh, thank you!" Mom replied.

When we got to his home, we met his wife, parents and child. They greeted us with warmth and they had us join them for dinner. After dinner, Mom called Dad and spoke to him in our own native tongue.

"We are in Philadelphia. We were able to get out of the airport without anybody knowing. Now we are in someone's home."

"I know a family over there. Let me give you their number and I will call them right after we hang up. Call them within a few minutes after you hang up with me," Dad answered.

"Ho ho."

Mom waited for five minutes before she called the phone number Dad gave her. "Hay, Sim talked to you. I don't know where I am. Talk to the guy who drove us here."

Mom asked the cab driver to talk to Dad's friend on the phone so he could give her directions to pick us up. "Mister, can you tell her how to get here?"

The lady came over that very night to pick us up and drove us to her home. We stayed with them for a couple of days before arrangements were made. We knew we couldn't fly into New York's airport because of what we had just experienced. So instead, we flew to Washington, D.C., then took a Greyhound bus to New York City.

My Special Friend

When we got to the New York City Port Authority bus terminal, a relative met us there and took us to his home. There I saw his wife Kim and his two children, my oldest brother Bo, and an old man with a wrinkled-up face sitting at the kitchen table, drinking and smoking.

When Kim and her children were in Hong Kong, they visited Aunty Ling's place as well and I would play with her son, Hokin, who was the same age as me, and her other child, who was older than me. I was saddened when they left and went to America to be with their father. I was left with no playmate.

It was a happy moment to see Hokin again, and we went off to our little world of imagination and games.

"You want to play hide and seek, Hokin?"

"Oh, I don't feel like playing that."

"You want to play arm wrestling?"

"I will beat you at that."

"Not if I beat you first."

"You're a girl. You can't beat me."

"You wanna bet?"

We put our arms on the coffee table and started wrestling.

"Hokin, quit intimidating her," his mother shouted from the dining room. Hokin got distracted by his mother so that I was able to push down his arm with full force.

"Ahahah, I beat you."

I thought Hokin was so cute back then that I had a crush on him during my preteen and teenager years, but I didn't tell anybody about it for fear of consequences. The feeling eventually faded away as I grew older.

It wasn't the way of my parents' generation or of our culture to talk about that: liking somebody, or thinking you liked somebody. If you had any inkling of liking someone, then it would turn into a marriage proposal. Besides, I wasn't a viable candidate to be anybody's wife with my crippling disease. Mom tried to keep my disease a secret so I wouldn't end up with no one wanting to marry me. Love wasn't the driving force for a marriage; marriage was merely a necessity to keep the family name alive.

Mom sat on the kitchen table and explained to the rest of the grown-ups how we escaped from the authorities. "Yee told the driver to take us to the bus station and from there, we hailed a Chinese cab driver."

"Very brave," Hokin's father declared with a smile.

"If it wasn't for Yee telling the driver to take us to a bus station, we wouldn't be here."

The old man who sat at the kitchen table never spoke a single word to me nor smiled at me. He kept drinking and smoking away. I stared at him intensely and wondered who he was. He looked like the picture I had of my father, I thought, but I wasn't sure. He was younger in the picture. No one introduced me to that man, nor did he introduce himself to me.

As evening came, we had dinner with Kim's family, then we went with my oldest brother and the old man to their place. I started to put two and two together and figured out that the old man was my father.

We took the M15 bus from Chinatown to 75th Street. We walked from the corner of 75th Street and First Avenue toward Second Avenue, but before we reached Second Avenue, we turned into a building and climbed two flights of stairs. The old man opened the apartment door and let us and Bo in.

As I passed through the hallway and into the kitchen, my tummy started to growl. "Mom, I am hungry."

The old man got furious with me and started yelling. "You just ate."

"She is a growing girl," Mom answered.

"Well, I am HUNGRY!" I told the old man.

"Is there food? I could cook her some."

"She just ATE," the old man retorted.

Tears started swelling in my eyes, that this old man who was supposed to be my father could turn out to be so cruel. Mom told me to deal with my hunger until the next day.

The next day Dad told Mom that she needed to work to pay back the money he spent on our trip. Slowly my hands and feet started to tremble, and soon I was having problems with walking again.

I went to a neighborhood school, P.S. 158. Although I liked it there, I had difficulty walking to school, and yet I lived too close for them to give me a school bus. So they transferred me to lower Manhattan P.S. 97 and put me in a Special Education class.

Someone told Mom about Bellevue Hospital, and she took me there to see a doctor. Since I was new to this country and hadn't grasped the English language yet, the hospital found a Chinese translator for us. The hospital had me see a neurologist, who examined me with the help of a Chinese translator. "Has anything catastrophic happened in her life?" the specialist asked.

"No," Mom told the translator. After careful examination, the doctor decided to have me admitted to the inpatient ward.

The staff placed me on a medical bed and wheeled me to a big empty room with multiple cubicle curtains and transferred me over to an electric hospital bed within the border of a hospital drape. There were a lot of empty beds and I was the only patient in that room until a Latino girl arrived. My mother wasn't too fond of her, for reasons I never understood; then again, my Mom griped to me about a lot of people she didn't like.

The Chinese translator came to visit me and brought me a coloring book, then escorted me to and from the children's play room. More than one translator came to visit me during my stay. One of them would become my special friend, Kent Cheung.

Kent was doing his internship there. He came to my hospital bed with one of the translators and introduced himself to me.

"Hi, I am Kent. How are you doing? I am here to help you through this."

I gave him a grin.

"You are an adorable little girl. I always wanted a little sister, but I got brothers."

Kent and I built a rapport instantly, and he did more than his job required of him. When Bellevue sent me to another building to have an MRI done, Kent was by my side. I had been scheduled to have an MRI when I first arrived at the hospital, but they hadn't been able to get an accurate result because of my uncontrollable movement, so this time, they put me under sedation.

When I woke up, Kent stroked his hand against my forehand and asked me if I was ok. I nodded. The feeling of being patted on and showered with his love made me feel special. Kent was kind, gentle, and supportive. He was a well-dressed and well-mannered gentleman in his early twenties who wore eyeglasses. His height was about 5 feet, 9 inches.

The Bellevue hospital had me undergo numerous tests, and Kent was there to support me through it all. The hospital diagnosed me with dystonia and prescribed me Tregretol. Unfortunately, the medicine didn't do anything for me, and I was still having problems with my movements.

After I was released from Bellevue, Kent and I kept in touch. He told me on the phone that he would come over and take me to Rockefeller Center. He came to our apartment to pick me up for my first Christmas holiday in New York.

Since I couldn't walk much, every step I took, my legs would wobble out of control and have a muscle spasm, so he would carry me in his arms. My mother went along with us.

We took the train to Rockefeller Center and when we got out of the subway station we saw a street vendor. "Do you want a pretzel?" Kent asked.

"Yeah," I responded happily.

My mother, being a very traditional Chinese woman, tried to prevent him from getting me a pretzel.

"No, no, no!" she insisted.

Kent, who understood my mother's culture, nonetheless disregarded her and got me the pretzel I wanted. The hot, salty aroma of the pretzel spread through the cold air, and it looked luscious to taste, so I broke a piece and put it into my mouth. This was my first pretzel, and it tasted pretty good.

When we walked to Rockefeller Center, the Christmas tree was all lit up between the ACA building and Prometheus' Statue, surrounded by an ice skating rink. There were people skating and enjoying the view of the gigantic Christmas tree about 75 feet high. The scenery was captivating, with the glimmer of life-sized angels shining brilliantly with tiny lights, and many other Christmas figures as well. The Christmas spirit was in the air; if I could only have eliminated my handicap, it would have been that much more enjoyable!

It was entertaining to be out to see this spectacular tree. Kent carried me in his arms the entire trip. He made me think that I was important enough for him to take me out, despite the nuisance of having to carry me in his arms. I felt warmth wrapped in Kent's arms.

After Kent took me home from our trip, I called him to see when he would come over again. "Can I speak to Kent?"

"He isn't home," his family member told me.

Soon after I hung up the phone, Mom told me not to bother Kent, that he was too busy to have time for me. What my mother said affected my psyche and put a dent in my relationship with Kent. Maybe Mom was right. Maybe Kent didn't want to see me again, and maybe he was too busy. Maybe that was why he didn't answer the phone--because he was avoiding me.

This made it harder for me to follow up with Kent. The last time I saw him, he took me to his father's toy store and the Bronx Zoo with his girlfriend. His girlfriend was one of the translators from the hospital. Later he sent me a card in the mail to let me know he got married to the lady that he was dating, but he didn't give me his current number. I looked at the address it was from and sent him a card at that address, but the mail got returned back to me. I was panicky that I had no way of getting hold of him. I double, triple, quadruple checked to see if I had gotten the sender's address written out correctly. I had.

I tried to bury the thought of him and moved on with my life. My mother was right: he was too busy for me. *I guess I wasn't as important as I thought I was.*

I didn't fully talk about him and the pain of losing him until I was in my early forties and had started working with a therapist. I burst out in tears in my session and told my therapist that he was the only person during that time who really cared about me. He gave me love, affection and attention that I never got from my family.

My therapist had me write a pretend letter to Kent to help me deal with my emotions. What would I say to him if I saw him? And this is my make-believe letter to him.

> Dear Kent,
>
> What happened to you? Why didn't you write your phone number down when you sent the card to me, letting me know that you married the girl you were dating. I sent you a card back but the card was sent back to me. I looked at the address on the card you sent to make sure it was the right address, and as far as I can tell, it was the right address. I was terrified of not being able to communicate with you. I thought you didn't want me anymore.

My mother told me you didn't have time for me because you were too busy, so I stopped trying to call your parents' phone numbers. I stopped trying to think you would care about me. As time went on, I got busy and didn't think much about you until I went to see a therapist in 2008.

I mentioned when I was a little girl there was this guy named Kent Cheung that really cared about me and how he told me that he always wanted a little sister. The last time I saw Kent was at the Bronx Zoo. He carried me in his arms when I was having a very difficult time walking. He was very supportive of me when I was going through various examinations in Bellevue. The therapist encouraged me to look for you by various means. I tried what she recommended but to no avail.

Most of the nights when everything is quiet, and I am lying in bed, I think of you. I thought maybe if I had kept your parents' number I could have asked them how to get hold of you. Or maybe I should have gotten help from the adults in school to help me find you when you sent me the card with your address on it. I wish I hadn't given up when I was a kid, but my mother told me that you were too busy for me, and I believed it.

Now I am 41, going on 42. I have regretted not having you in my life and in my growing up years. I wish you were there for me in my most miserable time with my family. The abuse and the neglect were heart-wrenching.

I don't know if you realized my father was an alcoholic. He abused me from time to time. He stopped financially supporting me and my mother when we came to this country. Being illegal immigrants and new to the country, my mother who was illiterate had to go to work in a sweatshop factory earning peanuts, working 12-13 hours a day to support the family, meanwhile leaving me home alone with my father.

My two older brothers never protected me from the abuse. One of them looked at me as if I deserved it. I hated how my brothers treated me. I hated that they never carried me when I was having a hard time walking. They didn't love me or care for me. My mother cared about me, but she was too caught up with how my father treated her. She never listened to me. Nobody listened to me.

I was very lonely without you. Why didn't you write back? Why didn't you call? I was just a kid. I needed you to be in my life in those times. I missed you so much. I am always reflecting on the memories I had of you—how you came with me when I had an MRI exam, and when I woke up from it, how you patted me on the head and asked me if I was ok. I still have the picture we took together in Rockefeller Center.

I don't know if I pushed you away, or if you got too busy with your married life. I just want

to be able to talk to you again and see what is
going on with you and to find out what happened
between us.

Love always,

Yee

As part of the letting go process, my therapist bought two
helium balloons and attached the letter to them and released
them into the air. The balloons and the letter got caught in
a tree.

Saved By God

My mother would often remind me how my oldest brother Bo used to give me a shoulder ride when we were in China and how I was his favorite. But that all changed when we were separated for five years, when Dad wanted Bo to come to America to be with him first. I think Bo suffered psychological abuse from Dad during that time, but nobody was willing to talk about it. One day Bo and Dad got into a verbal altercation, and Bo blurted out how awful Dad treated him.

Bo tried to spend time with me, but he already had his routine of life going and he didn't want to make any adjustment. So on his day off from work, he went out with his friends. He never took me out just to spend time with me.

Again I was left alone with my father and Forrest, and the abuse got worse. Once I was in the kitchen preparing a meal while my eyes were fixed on a TV show.

"*Iya*, watch what you're doing! You need to wait until the water is bubbly before you put in the meat. Pay attention to what you are doing."

I rolled my eyes in annoyance at him and continued with the way I was doing things.

"I told you, watch what you're doing," he shouted as he walked toward me. He grabbed my shoulder and shook me.

"Don't tell me what to do. I know what I am doing." I thrust his hands away from my shoulder.

He responded with quick and forceful shove that propelled me to the ground. My brother stood towering above me and stared at me with his eyebrows narrow and lips pursed. He didn't help me to get up from the ground but just went about his business.

Why can't you help me and be on my side? Why do you look at me as if it was my fault and I deserve to be smacked? Why can't you protect me?

I went to my room, crying my eyes out, but when my brother came in and saw me in my pitiful condition, he didn't try to comfort me or talk to me. He grabbed what he needed and closed the door behind him.

It was depressing to come home every day from school to face the abuser, with no one there to protect and support me, and no one to take me to the park to play with the other kids. I felt so isolated and secluded.

It seemed like the doctors in Bellevue were losing interest. I was seeing a different doctor every time I was there. I wanted to get better and I wanted help, but it just added to my depression that whenever I saw a different doctor, I would have to explain everything over again.

One day I went to Bellevue as usual for my neurology appointment and the doctor seemed to care about my condition. He had thin black hair with curly ends. His method of examination was unlike that of the other doctors, and he touched a part of my body that made me feel awkward.

"Here is my number, and if you have any problem, you can call me," he said with an accent.

No doctors had ever given me their personal office number. I thought he really cared and maybe he could help me to get better, so I called the number he gave me.

"I am still having problem with my legs and hands and they are not getting any better," I told the doctor.

"Why don't you come in so I can examine you and see if I could make it better?"

He had me meet him at his private office, and there wasn't anybody there. He told me to pull down my pants and he put his finger in my private area, and I got really uncomfortable and didn't know what to think. I looked up to see that his facial expression was composed and strict, and then I saw his forehead glisten with sweat.

I left his office feeling strange and uncomfortable and knowing something wasn't right, but I didn't know what it was and the word for it until I watched news broadcast about someone being sexually molested. Then it started to click and made sense. I had been molested by this doctor.

I went to my room and curled up in my bed, feeling disgusted. I thought he was different and he was going to help me to get better. How foolish I was. I felt there was no need to disclose what happened to me to my family. What was the point? They weren't there for me when I needed them. Up until today, they still have no idea about that incident. The feeling of being violated was horrendous. On top of the neglect, abandonment, and abuse by the people that I lived with, that I supposedly called family, this latest event just exacerbated my distress.

I prayed earnestly to Buddha to be able to walk, play, and run like any other kid. I did however many times of bowing that the Buddhist monk suggested to get my prayer answered. I did all the rituals that I was supposed to do, but I wasn't getting any better, just staying the same or sometimes getting worse.

It was a depressing and gloomy time of my life in which I saw no light at the end of the tunnel. Many times a month, I sobbed bitterly. I wanted to end this misery. Who would know and who would care? I wish I never would have come to American to meet my Dad. Life was better in Hong Kong.

In my junior high years I did plan to end my life. One weekend all the members of the family had gone out and left me home alone. I decided it was a good opportunity to end my misery without anybody's intervention. I didn't like blood; it grossed me out to think of sticking a knife inside me to kill myself, so I planned something less gruesome.

I turned off the pilot light in the middle of the stove and turned on each of the stove burners. I closed all the windows and I sat in my bed for hours, purposefully inhaling the gas, but I wasn't getting any symptoms of poisoning.

Eventually my neighbors started knocking on my door because they smelled the gas. I got nervous so I turned everything off and put things back in order. I didn't want to have to explain anything to my neighbors so I ignored the door knock. Eventually they figured that no one was home so they ceased knocking.

That wasn't the end of my suicide attempts. I continued to plan on less intrusive methods to end this despondency. I went to a neighborhood drug store and browsed through some pills. I had seen a TV show where this character was able to end her life with sleeping pills. I came to a sleeping pill section, took the box from the shelf, and read the instructions. I pondered deeply as I stood there. *I think this should do it.*

I hid the bottle from my family and methodically planned my suicide without anyone suspecting. The only person I worried about was my mother. She would be devastated if she discovered that I killed myself, so I wrote a letter to her. In that letter I told her that it wasn't her fault and I loved her, but I had been just so miserable with my life, and I hoped she could understand what I was going through.

The night I was preparing to take my sleeping pills, my mother was home. She could tell I was gloomy and tried to find out what was wrong, but I withdrew from her. I didn't want her to change my mind.

Why did you me leave me home all alone with him? Why didn't you protect me from him? Why didn't you listen to my cry? You weren't there when I needed you. Why didn't you leave him and quit worrying what other people might say? You worry more about what other people think than my safety. Why did you come back and put up with him again? What about our safety while living with this destructive man who didn't care about any of his family members? I can't put up with this anymore. I need to end this destructive life that I have been living in. I just couldn't see any way out except to take my life.

In my suicide letter to my mother, I didn't write all my inner turmoil. It would destroy her. I hid the letter by my bedside.

I went out in the kitchen to get a cup of water and went back to my room and closed the door behind me. No one else was in the room except me. I took the whole bottle of the sleeping pills and went to sleep. *This was it and I wouldn't have to suffer anymore.*

The irony of the story was I woke the next day bright and early with no negative side effect of ingesting an enormous number of the sleeping pills. I woke up feeling furious that I was still alive. Yet a shred of light came into my soul, and somehow I knew there was a God of this universe who created heaven and earth, you and me, and kept me alive for a purpose, but frankly I didn't know what that was. I started to call out to him.

"Why are you doing this to me? Why are you keeping me alive? I don't want to live anymore. How could you do this to me? God, are you out there? Are you real? If you are real, show me who you are."

My purpose right now was to find out who this God was and why he thought I should live.

My Awards

I went from P.S. 97 elementary school to Intermediate School 70 (I.S. 70), also known as O. Henry school, named after the author O. Henry, who wrote "The Gift of the Magi" and other short stories. It was located between 8th and 9th Avenues on 17th Street in Chelsea.

Some of the students from P.S. 97 went to the same junior high I went to. I didn't know why the others weren't there. Did they get to pick out a different school to go to? Or maybe their parents were involved in their lives that they made sure their kids go to the school they wanted or a school close by them. Nobody asked me if I wanted to go to O. Henry. They just sent me there. I didn't know if I had a choice in it.

My junior high teacher, Mrs. Sylvia Spellum, was a white lady with short straight brown hair with curled ends who wore designer frame glasses. She saw that I was a hard worker and my grades excelled above other students in her class, so she placed me in some mainstream classes instead of having all my classes with the Special Ed students. Two of my mainstream classes were math and typing. Despite my physical and mental hardships at home, studying was one of the ways to escape from it all. I was on the honor roll every semester.

When our class broke for lunch, we rushed to the cafeteria to get in line for food. After we had been served, the students scattered to different tables. I saw some Asian Americans sitting at one of the tables, so I bought my lunch tray to where they were and sat near them.

"Hi, what is your name?" I tried to break the ice.

"I am LeeAnne and this is my sister Wei."

"Hi, I am Yee. What grade are you in?"

"We are in the eighth grade."

"Oh, so am I. Do you speak another language?"

"Yes! We do."

"What do you speak?"

"We speak Cantonese."

"Ohhh, I do too. Are you from Hong Kong?"

"Yeah."

I got uneasy as the conversation progressed for fear of them asking me what classroom I was in. I didn't want to have to tell them that I was in Special Ed. Other kids would tease those of us that were in Special Ed for being stupid. I didn't want them to think that way about me, so I got frigid with them and abruptly ended the conversation.

"It was nice meeting you, but I have to get back to class. There is some extra work I have to do."

As time went on, I continued to hang out with them during lunch. They were nice to me overall and maybe they knew I was in Special Ed despite my disguise. As I got to know them better, I was comfortable enough to tell them what classroom I was in, but I never told them it was a Special Ed class. They became my regular lunch period friends.

One lunch period as I got my lunch plate and headed to our usual table, there was a new girl sitting with them, and I wondered who that was.

"This is Kathy, Yee," LeeAnne introduced me to the new girl as I approached their table.

"Hi Yee.

"Hi Kathy."

"Yee, that is a Chinese name. Isn't it?" Kathy declared.

"Yeah."

"Well, is there an English name you want to be called?"

I thought for a moment, then I said, "Yeah, I think I'd like to be called Cindy."

"Then that will be your English name and we'll call you Cindy from now on."

"Hi Cindy," LeeAnne said with a smile.

After we finished our lunch, we split up and went to our classes. "Bye Cindy!" they all said in unison with a giggle.

"Bye."

That name Cindy spread through my class and the entire school. They even gave me my honor certititicate with my nickname Cindy on it.

"Cindy, I am having a birthday party and you can come," one of my classmates, Ramona, announced.

"O.K. Give me your number."

Ramona went to the same elementary school with me and now we were in the same junior high school. She was a gentle and soft-spoken girl with short curly brown hair. She got sick a lot from her asthma and had a lot of absences. When she was in school, she sat with me in most of the classes and listen to my rambles. She didn't talk much but she was a good listener.

When I got home, I called Ramona to get more information on her birthday party.

"Hi, can I speak to Ramona?

"Hold on. Ramona, you got a call," her brother shouted from the background.

Ramona came on the line. "Hello!"

"Hi Ramona, how're things going?"

"Oh, it is O.K. What is going on with you?"

"Hey, when is the party and where is it?"

"It is at my place and it is next Saturday." Then she gave me directions to her place.

"I don't know if I can make it. There is something going on that day." I didn't want her to know that I had nobody to take me there and I didn't understand her directions. It was hard for me to go anyplace all by myself with my arduous walking.

I didn't broadcast to any of my friends when I went for my honor roll ceremonies every semester. All the honor rollees sat in the auditorium as the principal announced the students' names, gave them an award certificate, and shook their hands for good work. I feared my fellow friends would put me down and think that I might be pompous. Nobody knew about my home life, and I was too ashamed to tell anyone about it.

At my junior high school graduation, my teacher, Mrs. Spellum, nominated me for awards given by the New York Board of Education Division of Special Education and the president of the borough of Manhattan, David Norman Dinkins, for surmounting above other students in my class.

Back in the apartment, I told Mom about the Board of Education ceremony but not the Manhattan borough president award. "Mom, I am going to be given an award for my good grades."

"Oh, when is it?"

"It is in June, the same day as my graduation."

"We'll have to see if we can go."

I don't think Mom told everybody in the household about my ceremony, but she told Forrest about it, so he could drive me to the event. When we got to the event place, a reporter from the *China Daily News* greeted us and told us that he was going to publish an article about me. It was a joyous occasion for me to have this plaque awarded to me, to receive the $500 cash award as well, and to be published in the *China Daily News*. I felt a sense of accomplishment.

The reporter interviewed everybody that was present: my teacher and the school principal, my mother, Forrest, and me.

It appeared that my brother Forrest was happy for me but he didn't say any positive words to me. After the award and my graduation ceremonies, I had a big smile on my face with a sense of pride, but my brother Forrest gave me a disapproving look for feeling the way I did. His look crushed my spirit.

Forrest got the paper on the day it was printed and read the article. Dad showed the paper to our neighbors and called his friends about it.

Kim's daughter just happened to pick up the paper and came to my article before we told them about it.

"Oh, my gosh. This is horrible news. Mom, look at this paper."

Kim read the article and knew it was talking about me. "I can't believe the paper said that. It will ruin her chances of ever finding a husband."

Kim was concerned that the article mentioned my disability, so without hesitation she felt it was her duty to warn my mother about my future.

She dialed our home phone number and Mom picked up the phone.

"Do you know what the papers are saying? Now the whole world is going to know your daughter can't walk and nobody will want her," Kim said.

Mom's spirit got crushed by Kim; she couldn't say anything positive back to her, but just agreed with her. Mom stopped feeling proud of me and told me what Kim said. I felt so ashamed of my award that I threw the newspaper away.

I called the Manhattan borough president's office and told them I wouldn't be attending the ceremony, and they told me they will mail me the certificate.

Again in my later years, in my early forties when I started to deal with my emotional baggage, I told one of my therapists about my award and how ashamed I felt. The therapist told me to bring the awards in to her and told me that I should be proud of myself. She also encouraged me to find that article.

It took me years of research to find it. A librarian from Columbia University told me that there wasn't any microfilm for that year, but I chose to believe otherwise and persevered in finding it. Back then, no one had ever told me what the article actually said, but this time around I was going to find out. So I had my friend translate it into English for me. I put my awards and the newspaper article with the English translation alongside it in a frame on the wall of my home office.

This is the article that was translated.

Cindy Yee Kong

Yee Kong, a top student in the New York, overcame physical disability by perseverance and combined with industriousness.

Six years ago, Yee Kong, a nine-year-old girl with serious muscle atrophy in her mouth and legs, immigrated to the USA from Hong Kong with her whole family. People were worried about this wretched girl with limp legs because she could not speak Chinese well, not to speak of English. They were concerned her future in the USA.

Six years later, on June 17, Yee Kong, a ninth grade student, received a prize and $500 from Stanford Memorial Fund at 3 pm in the auditorium of the New York Education Department. She was nominated with other three American students with physical disabilities because she got all As in all courses in the past three years. All of them not only were the top students among 14,000 students with physical disabilities, but also exceptional among all students in New York City.

It was a simple ceremony with few people on that day. Accompanied by her parent and brother, Yee arrived at the auditorium. Stanley Witty, president of New York Sixth Middle School where Yee studied; Mr. Belo, a consultant in special education; and Mrs. Spellum, Yee's teacher, all arrived in series. Yee talked merrily to them in fluent English.

The reporter asked how she could master English as a second language so well in such a short six-year period by overcoming her obstacle in speaking. "Do not be shy, just talk with your classmates," she replied with a short answer. Spellum, her teacher, told that she loved to study and had a strong desire to learn something. She had a good relationship with classmates and was favored by all teachers.

Her mother was a shy woman. She said her daughter studied hard at home. As an illiterate person, she is glad to support her daughter in her studies and wishes her a bright future.

When talking to her about her future, Yee said she will study at Mabel Dean Bacon High School and will take business and education courses. She likes mathematics very much. She is planning to study computer as her major in college.

My High School Years

After junior high I went to Mabel Dean Beacon Vocational High School in hope to study in business and education. It was small building with only a cramped space for students to move around between classes.

Forrest found a location in New London, Connecticut, to start a Chinese takeout restaurant business. Mom moved with him to Connecticut to help him with the restaurant work. Mom learned how to cook fried rice and egg foo young, and to perform other restaurant responsibilities. Dad went along with them because he wanted someone to buy him beer and pay the bills. He didn't want to risk staying in New York and end up having to pay the bills.

Although I had a neighbor downstairs that I could go to for help if I needed to, I was living in the apartment all by myself. Bo had gotten married and lived in Chinatown. After weeks of attending my high school, I was having a hard time understanding my teachers and I didn't like the school. This killed all my inspiration on the subject I intended to study. I wanted a change of school and to leave New York, so I called Mom one evening.

"Mom, I am having blood in my stool."

"Are you making yourself soup every night?"

"No!"

"Oh my, no wonder you are having a problem. You need to move in here with us so I could cook you a home-cooked meal and soup every night."

"All right."

I just needed Mom to tell me that I could move in with her. I didn't know why I couldn't blatantly say to her that I missed her and I didn't want to live all by myself. Maybe being honest with our feelings was not part of our family norm.

My brother picked me up from New York and drove me to New London, Connecticut. The next morning Mom and I went to a new school to enroll. I walked slowly, dragging my feet as we opened one of the school doors which led to a gym. There was a teacher holding a class lesson who saw us meandering.

"Can I help you?" the teacher asked.

I stopped and walked over to where he was and told him I was here to enroll for school. He told me how to get to the admission office. Being enrolled in New London High School was a very easy process.

"What school did you go to before?" the admission counselor inquired.

"I went to Mabel Dean Bacon High School in New York."

"All right. Did you have anything from your last school?"

"Yes. Here is my report card from my junior high."

"All right. We just need to fill out some paperwork and get you started for school."

They placed me in regular classes. I was afraid that they would put me in Special Ed. Class, so I neglected to tell them that I was in Special Ed. in junior high. Even though my report card said I was in a health class (that was a nice way of saying

I was in Special Ed.), they either overlooked it or didn't know the meaning behind it.

I wasn't in Special Ed. when I attended Mabel Dean Beacon. I had a choice after graduating from junior high of what high school I want to go to and whether I wanted to be in regular classes. New London wasn't as cramped as Mabel Dean Bacon. It was a big facility with plenty of space for the students to maneuver from one class to another without having to collide with each other.

During lunch period, as I sat behind a table with my lunch tray, an Asian girl came up and initiated a conversation.

"Hi, I am Thuy. What's yours?"

"My name is Cindy."

"Are you new here?"

"Yes, I am."

"Where did you move from?"

"New York."

"Oh!"

"What about you? Where are you from?"

"I am from Vietnam."

Thuy and I begun our new friendship. She had two younger sisters who also attended New London High. She was the oldest in the family. She would pick me up from my house and bring me to school every day.

One day Thuy dropped me off at my brother's restaurant. Forrest was reading a newspaper in the customers' dining area about the new law on hiring illegal immigrants. The Immigration Reform and Control Act of 1986 stated that it was illegal for employers to hire undocumented immigrants and deemed it to be criminal. My brother got panicky about the new law, since all his employees were undocumented, as were we. He was afraid his business wouldn't survive under this new regulation, so he decided to sell the restaurant and move back to New York. I shared my family's plan of moving back to New York with Thuy.

"You know you can stay with us and finish off your tenth grade year," Thuy offered.

"Oh, really?"

"Yeah, I will talk to my parents and we could work something out."

It worked out that I was able to stay with Thuy's family and finished out my year. Mom sent them room and board money every month.

After staying with Thuy's family for a while, my relationship with Thuy changed. She stopped talking with me and avoided me at all costs. I didn't know what I did to cause her to act this way toward me. Despite my best efforts to talk to her, she would evade me.

Thuy's two sisters who were of elementary age secretly shared with me the reason Thuy and their older sisters didn't talk to me anymore. "My older sisters didn't like that you wore your clothes more than once before you wash them," they said. "They think you have a hygiene problem."

They were a bit more affluent than us, and they did things differently than we would do them. They lived in a beautiful 800- to 900-square foot house, with a spacious living area and amenities like a laundry machine, a nice big yard, a laundry room, private bathrooms, kitchen, dining area, and living room.

Yes, it I felt it was a no-win battle with Thuy and her sisters to tell them otherwise. It was true what they said about me wearing my clothes more than once, but I was not a filthy person. If they came out of the lifestyle I came from, I think they would do the same as well. They were shallow and superficial.

So I passed my time talking to their younger sisters, eventually moving my bed and my belongings to their room and becoming their roommate. Being away from my parents and living in a rural environment improved my physical condition. I was at a point where I wasn't having any muscle spasms. I didn't have the stress of dealing with my father's abuse, and the hustle and bustle of New York life. New London was a seaport city with fresher air from the bay.

After I finished tenth grade, I moved back to New York, and slowly the symptoms of my disease began to creep up again. I called my friend LeeAnne to find out what high school she was attending and if her school was appropriate for me to go to. She told me that she went to Bayard Rustin High School for the Humanities, and it was just a couple blocks away from our junior high. She thought it was a decent school. I went there during summer break to enroll in class.

It was a long wait, and the school personnel weren't as nice as the people in Connecticut. I spent the whole day waiting in line with other students to talk to the admission counselor. When it was my turn, he scrutinized my previous Special Ed. class and gave me a hard time about placing me in regular classes. But I told him I was in regular classes in New London High. Why should I have to be in the Special Ed. class at Bayard? "I was able to get As and Bs in New London High School. Why wouldn't I able to do well in this school?" I debated with him. Finally I was able to persuade him that I would do well in regular classes.

The beginning of the school year arrived, and we had a half day on the first day of school. I went to the classroom that I was assigned to during my enrollment, and the teacher passed out our class schedules and our transportation passes. This classroom was our homeroom class, where we were to come every day after our first period for the teacher to take attendance, give an announcement, and give us our monthly transportation passes.

I developed a routine of the route I took to school. I took the M15 bus from 75th Street on 2nd Avenue to 14th Street, and then transferred to a cross-town bus to 8th Avenue. As I waited at the bus station on 14th Street, I saw a girl standing there who looked familiar. She had long, straight, dark brown hair below her shoulders. We both got on the same bus when it arrived.

"Are you in my homeroom?" I asked her as we found our seats in the bus.

"What homeroom are you in?"

"Mrs. Ritterman's."

"Oh, yes. That is my homeroom too. I didn't know you were in my homeroom."

"Oh, yes. I am."

"Well, what is your name?"

"Cindy. What's yours?"

"My name is Lydia."

The bus came to our stop and we both got off and walked toward our school; then we split up and went to our first period class. After first period, I saw Lydia in the homeroom and started to talk to her. "Hey, what are you doing after school?" she queried.

"I will be going home."

"You want to come and play badminton with my friends?"

"I don't know. I don't know how to play it."

"You don't know how? I could show you how."

I showed up to the after-school curriculum program and found Lydia playing badminton with her friends, so I stayed briefly. She tried to show me how to play the game, but I wasn't grasping it. Later she discovered that I never had done any gym or any physical activities because of my involuntary leg and hand movement.

Lydia and I started to do things together after school. I came to find out that her father was half Chinese, half American, and her mother was fully Chinese. Her father grew up in an orphanage in Taiwan, and he had never known his parents. He was fluent in Mandarin but not in English.

She invited me to her home where she cooked me a Taiwan-style home cooked meal. Then eventually I let the cat out of the bag and told her about my problems at home and my disease.

"God can heal you," she declared. "You should come to my church."

Her statement gave me hope, and hope was something I was searching for. I prayed to God in front of the window of my bedroom, "God, if that's you, show me the way." Minutes after I prayed, I called Lydia. "What are you doing tomorrow?" she asked.

"Oh, nothing!"

"You want to come to my church?"

"Sure."

We met at Union Square and took the F train to Far Rockaway in Queens, then we walked to her church. In her church, I learned about the saving grace message of Jesus Christ and accepted him into my life and made him my savior. Gradually I was able to use my four extremities without any twitching majority of the time.

Graduation

One of the milestones of my last year in high school was applying for permanent resident status. In 1986, President Reagan passed the Immigration Reform and Control Act. This Act not only criminalized employers who hired undocumented residents; it also stated that anybody who had been in this country before 1982 could apply for a green card. This law granted amnesty to nearly 3 million illegal immigrants, and we were part of that 3 million. Although the law passed in November of 1986, my family didn't apply until 1989. That was the year we gathered all the necessary documents to prove that we were here before 1982.

"Yee, give me all your report cards so I can bring them to the law office and have them make copies," Mom screamed from the kitchen.

"Give me a chance to put it together, and I will get it to you," I replied.

Mom and my brothers asked their employers to write a letter stating that they had been working for them before 1982. I gathered all my report cards and gave them to Mom.

With this amnesty law passed, I was able to get a social security number, which helped me to apply for college and college financial aid. I was afforded a chance to have a better life than the illegal immigrants had led.

In some ways I was a typical teenager. I would sing and dance along in my room to the popular songs of the 80s, like Michael Jackson's "Beat It" or "Billie Jean"; Cyndi Lauper's "Girls Just Want To Have Fun"; Olivia Newton John's, "Physical"; Salt N- Pepa's "Push It"; and The Jets' "Crush on You." Michael Jackson's moonwalk was growing in popularity back then, and the teens would try to mimic it. And yes, I had tried it as well in the privacy of my own room! Unfortunately I couldn't get the flow of the dance. One day I turned on the stereo and blasted the song "Beat It."

> *They told him don't you ever come around here*
> *Don't wanna see your face, you better disappear*
> *The fire's in their eyes and their words are really clear*
> *So beat it, just beat it*
>
> *You better run, you better do what you can*
> *Don't wanna see no blood, don't be a macho man*
> *You wanna be tough, better do what you can*
> *So beat it, but you wanna be bad*
>
> *Just beat it, beat it, beat it, beat it*
> *No one wants to be defeated*
> *… Just beat it, beat it*
> *Just beat it, beat it*
> *Just beat it, beat it*
> *Just beat it, beat it*

All of a sudden my Dad screamed behind the closed door. "Turn that music down," he barked.

I rolled my eyes and turned the music down. "Gosh, I can't even play my music," I whispered under my breath.

"See, all your daughter does is listen to American music. She doesn't do anything in the apartment. You raise your daughter bad," Dad screeched at Mom.

"I raise my daughter bad? What about you? She is not just my daughter," Mom answered.

"You don't know how to raise your daughter to be good. You raise a bad daughter." Dad picked up his beer can and slammed it against the table.

Mom and Dad's constant bickering had made me think seriously about going away for college and this fight had pushed me over the edge. "Hell with it. I am going away," I thought. I didn't think I could focus on my studies if I stayed home. I needed to get away from them and from this toxic environment.

The next day at school, the students huddled outside the school building before the start of the first period. There was a group of cool kids wearing black and white clothing gathered on the corner. Hairstyles during that time were big and had an unnatural appearance. These cool kids used a lot of spray to make their hair stand up and look bulky.

When I walked past them, one of the them in the crowd saw me wearing faded blue jeans with blue sketches of flowers on them and sneered at me. Yeah, they were the cool kids with the cool clothes and hair that I couldn't afford to do or buy.

We were too poor to get name brand clothes like Gap or Banana Repbulic. I wore what had been given to me, and if somebody didn't like it, then it was too bad for them. I was not going to make my mother spend everything she worked hard for to put food on the table, and a roof over our head, to buy me name brand clothes so I could fit in with the cool crowd. I ignored his stare, and continued walking.

I went to my first period class and after that all the students gathered in their designated homerooms. I saw Lydia and approached her in homeroom. "Lydia, you want to go away for college? We could apply to State University of New York (SUNY) schools," I said.

"Yeah, we can room together and stuff. Let's go for it."

"Let's pick up the application between classes at the guidance counselor's office, or I could pick it up tomorrow morning."

"O.K. Hey, there is a new student over there. I will go over and say hi to him," Lydia said.

It turned out this new student was from Thailand and over a period of time they became a couple. He sure knew how to sweep Lydia off her feet. Lydia giggled at the slightest things this boy said or did. Whether he tapped his finger on the bridge of her nose at a cafeteria table or the simple words he uttered such as "hi," it was like she was living in a pink cloud. She was far from reality.

The next day I went to school, with a scratch mark on my chin, to pick up SUNY college application from my guidance counselor's office.

"What happened to your face?" the guidance counselor interrogated.

"My Dad hits me."

"Are you O.K.?"

"Yes!"

He started filling out papers on his desk, and it turned out that he was arranging for me to see a school counselor through

80

the rest of the school year. The school counselor picked me up from one of my classes and took me to her office to talk about whatever was on my mind. I enjoyed being away from classes and having someone listening to me. That was "my time." "I am afraid of going to college," I told her. "I don't know if I will make it."

"You don't need to be afraid. You can make it. It is not that hard."

"Really?" I smiled, with an ounce of hope.

What she said reaffirmed my confidence, and it stayed with me throughout my college years. When I was having a challenge in my studies, I would rehearse what she said in my mind.

During homeroom period, Lydia and I looked at the list of SUNY schools and gave our top three choices of schools we qualified for on the applications. We filled out the rest of the applications and mailed them out. In due time, we got acceptance letters from SUNY Farmingdale on Long Island. After we got the letters, we both filled out the application to be roommates together.

We were all set to go to college and be roomies until Lydia told me in church that she couldn't handle being away on her own. She felt she would go bonkers with her freedom, so she needed to stay home to have boundaries. I was shocked and disappointed that I was going to have to do this all on my own.

Lydia's boyfriend was whispering in her ears during lunch period. "Oh, come on, baby. Just one time for me. We are graduating." He kissed her forehead softly.

"Hee, hee, hee," Lydia chuckled bashfully.

A few weeks later during a church service I saw a pastor pull Lydia aside and point his finger at her with a degrading demeanor. Lydia lowered her head in humility and accepted the pastor's reprimand.

It turned out that Lydia gave herself to her boyfriend and after he got what he wanted, he threw her on the sidelines. The church members showed their disfavor toward her. She felt so afflicted by their persecution and the emotional anguish of being dumped that she finally lashed out with her shameful secret of being molested by her father; however, she didn't get any sympathy, understanding, or compassion from anyone in the congregation. They continued to put her down. The way they treated her really disturbed me.

I didn't get a cap and gown and a yearbook from high school because I wasn't willing to spend close to one hundred dollars for it, although my mother was willing to pay it, and neither did Lydia. We sat in the audience at our graduation ceremony instead of being in the graduating class on the front rows. At the end of the ceremony, the graduating class threw their caps in the mid-air and shouted a cheer. We met our friends outside the building and took some pictures afterward.

Before you knew it, summer break breezed right past me, and it was time for college. I gathered the little bit of clothes that I had and packed them in a vinyl sport bag that Mom and I used when we came to America. A lady in church named Peggy arranged someone to drive me to Farmingdale for my first day of school. They also picked me up every Friday afternoon to take me back to the city so I could go to church on Saturday morning, and took me back to school on Sunday evening.

Freshman in College

I approached my first night in the college dormitory with almost paralyzing fear. I didn't know what to expect going to a place I hadn't been before and living with people I didn't know, but one thing I know was I could trust God on this and I was going to be O.K.

A man from church named Wayne stayed with me during the dormitory check-in process. I checked in at the front lobby and got my keys and room number from the residential staff. We went one flight of stairs, found my room number, and opened the door.

There was a gigantic horizontal sliding window facing me as I opened the door, and one bed in each corner of the room, with closets at the end of the bed. In the middle, there were two study tables facing each other with bedside cabinets beneath them. My roommate hadn't showed up yet and I was curious to find out who she was going to be.

Up and down the hallway were rooms filled with other students that I had yet to meet. There was one big bathroom with multiple toilet stools and showers that we all shared. We only had one public phone at the end of the hallway.

I checked in on the weekend before the school week to get settled in. Wayne from church asked if I was going to be O.K.

"Yeah!" I replied and took a deep breath.

"I will pick you up Friday for church. See you then."

"O.K."

He headed out of my room, down the stairs, and his figure eventually disappeared. I stood there motionless for a few seconds trying to figure out what I should do next. I got out my mattress cover and pillow cover to get my bed ready for the night's rest and I spread my blanket out as well. I sprawled on my bed and wondered what I needed to do. *I am starting to get a bit hungry. Where is the cafeteria?* I wondered.

Then I looked at the brochure that I got from the residential staff to see where it was, but I was having a hard time understanding the map, so I asked another fellow student in the hallway how to find the cafeteria. "You go down the staircase and walk straight out this front door and then you will see it," she answered.

"Oh, thanks."

"'No problem."

I followed her instruction and found the cafeteria. I got a tray of food from the servers and I circled my eyes around the room trying to figure out whom I could sit and mingle with. I saw a girl who was sitting alone eating her meal, so I went to her table and sat across from her.

She was African American. I was fed by my family the negative stereotype of a "black ghost," as they called them. "They are no good. They will attack and rob you. You can't trust a black ghost." I had seen some parents using the "black boogie man" as a scare tactic to get their kids to finish their meal. "You better finish this meal or the black boogie man is coming to get you."

Even though I was hesitant to find out for myself whether what I was told about black people was true or not, I was able to muster some courage to discover that on my own instead of being closed minded. "Hi, can I sit here?" I asked her.

"Sure," she said with an accent I couldn't identify.

"What is your name?"

"My name is Letty. What's yours?"

"My name is Cindy. Are you new here?"

"No! This year is my second year. Are you new?"

"Yeah! I don't know where everything is."

"I could show you around. It is not that hard."

After we ate our meals, we walked back to our dorm. I showed Letty where I lived so she knew how to find me and Letty showed me where she was staying as well. She stayed in a different building than me. She lived in a single room building that she had applied for, and there was a waiting list to get a room there. It turned out that Letty was an Ethiopian.

"Wow, Letty you don't have a roommate. I wish I got your room."

Letty smiled at my remark. "You got your class schedule. I will show you where the buildings are, so tomorrow you will know where to go for your classes."

Letty showed me the location of the buildings of my classes but I was too overwhelmed to take it all in.

The next morning I walked to my first class but I wasn't sure exactly where it was, so I asked people along the way to make sure I was on the right path.

I wasn't allowed to cook in my dorm, so my mother brought me a small rice cooker so I could heat up a can of soup or instant noodles for late night hunger. Letty could cook in her building and her resident had a kitchen on the first floor. From time to time she would invite me and her other friend Suka to have a meal in her room.

I made it through the first week of classes. Everything was new to me: new environment, new peers, new school, new living conditions, new learning environment, and new levels of academic work. I was inundated with these changes coming at me all at once and I was hoping my mother would call me up to see how I was doing, but she didn't. I needed to be strong and focus so I could get my bachelor degree in four years.

Wayne picked me up early on Friday evening and drove me back to the city. On Saturday morning after the church service, I told Peggy that I didn't want to come back to the city next Saturday.

"Cindy, you need to come to church every week."

I just didn't want to come next week. I wanted to stay in school.

"No, no, no, you come to church next Saturday."

"You know what, I don't want to come next Saturday or the Saturday after that or ever after that. Don't tell me what I need to do."

Her jaw dropped, and she was so taken aback by my statement that she pulled herself back a little. "Cindy, you never talked to me like this."

"That is because you never saw my other side."

I was tired of this church telling me how to live my life and if that was how churches were then I didn't want anything to do with it. I didn't want some religious organization telling me what to do and what to believe in. I believe in you, God, but I don't want to go to church.

I met one of Letty's building mates, Tieh, who lived downstairs from her. Tieh lived in a part of the building that was for male residents only. Tieh was a Chinese-Vietnamese American. Through him I was able to know other Asian Americans on campus.

In the cafeteria, I saw a petite girl, about 4'9" or less, with a short haircut that at first made me think she was a boy. Tieh sat at a table with his Vietnamese friends. "What do you think that person's gender is? Is it he or she?" Tieh and his friends tried to figure out.

I sat nearby her to see if I could erase this myth. "Hi, how're you doing?" I stated.

"Oh, hi. How are you doing?" she smiled. As soon as she opened her mouth to speak, it was clear that she was a female.

"Are you new?"

"Yeah, I am."

"So am I."

"That is neat."

"Which dorm are you staying at?"

We had a friendly conversation and I came to find out that she lived in the same building as me but on the opposite side. Her name is Beatrice and she was a Japanese American. We hung out together often.

My roommate finally showed up. She was a Jamaican. "Hey mon, how yuh doing?" she said.

I smiled and welcomed her. We got along as roommates but we weren't buddies. Occasionally we'd go to dinner together. She had her group of friends and I had mine. We respected each other boundaries.

In our room one evening she shared a rumor that had been circulated among her friends. "Yo, Cindy, people hers been passing rumor bout yuh an Beatrice. Since yuh two hers no mon, they said yur are gay."

I certainly didn't know how to respond to what she said. Yes, I never had a man in my life up to this point, but I do like men and it was just that I hadn't found one or been pursued by one—and besides, my studies came first.

Once I did a foolish thing that hurt my friendship with Beatrice. We were walking down the stairs from her room to the front lobby and there was a pizza delivery boy who was trying to find the room he needed to get his pizza to. Beatrice was nice enough to help him out and showed him where he needed to go. I looked at Beatrice and smiled and said loudly in front of the delivery boy, "You like him, don't you?"

Even though I meant it to be funny, my statement embarrassed her so much that she blushed. Little by little she made excuses whenever I visited her to hang out. "Oh Cindy, I got a lot of work to do. I really need to study."

Back then I couldn't figure what I did wrong to make her stop talking to me, but now I am older, I know why. What I said was very inconsiderate, rude and childish. I mortified her in front of the pizza delivery boy.

A girl named Wendy, who lived off campus, started an Asian Association Club for Asian Americans to get together to socialize and have fun. She coordinated different recreational activities throughout my freshman year. One of the events that she put together was a roller-skating event that was open to everyone, not just Asians.

In the roller-skating rink, the Asian Association Club covered the rental expense of the rollerskates. I didn't know how to rollerskate, but I put on the shoes in hope that someone will help me. Some of the people in the group did help me in the beginning, but after a little while holding me, it started to be too much and they passed me off from one person to the next.

A guy named Yuon saw that I was having problems, and he started to approach me in the rink and asked me if I needed help. As I tried terribly to keep my upper body in sync with my legs, unfortunately my legs moved faster than my body and I started to tumble. I reached out my hands to him and hollered "yahh!" He grabbed hold of my hand and kept me from falling. He spent the rest of the night helping me in the rink so I wouldn't fall as often. He was an African American with broad shoulders and a ponytail down the back of his neck.

Toward the end of the night, when it was time for the group to head back to campus, I said, "Thanks for helping me, Yuon."

"Sure no problem! Hey, what building do you live in and what is your room number?"

I told him the information he asked for.

The next day I got a knock on my door. I opened the door and found him standing outside. "Hey, how is it going? Come on in."

He had a big smile on his face and asked if I was doing O.K. with all the falling over I did last night.

"Oh, I have some bruises in my legs and ass, otherwise I am O.K," I smiled.

"Hey, we should hang out, you know. You want to go out for a ride on my bike sometime?"

"Sure."

As it turned out, we begun dating, and shortly after that he had an unusual remark to say to me. "I want to have sex with you," he declared.

Sex? I was shocked to hear that. I know nothing about that subject. I told him I don't want to get pregnant.

"You won't get pregnant. I will do a withdrawal." This is the worst method of protection, as I learned later in life. Thanks God I didn't get pregnant through his and my stupidity.

My conscience told me it was wrong to have sex before marriage but I didn't have anything to base it on. I went to a school therapist in hope that she could affirm my conscience.

"My boyfriend wants to have sex with me," I commented.

"Well, are you ready for it?"

"Well, no!'

"Then tell him that you are not ready."

The therapist's remark led me to believe it was O.K. to have sex. It was a matter of readiness. Eventually we did it, and in the heat of the moment it felt good, but I was left with a guilty conscience afterward. I prayed to God to remove this sexual desire from me.

The Assault

I think God ordained sex in a marital setting primarily for the purpose of protecting our emotional well-being. In a marriage, there would be a sense of commitment toward each other. I think women get emotionally tangled up with someone through sex, and if the person you were engaging in sexual intercourse with is not your spouse, then you are emotionally vulnerable.

Yuon broke up with me after few months of dating. I was extremely heartbroken and I would do anything to be with him again. His sisters and mother, who adored me, tried to get us back together. Their plan was to turn me into an attractive young lady with proper clothing and makeup.

One of his sisters Jahil, took me to Bloomingdale's to have a makeover and shopped for clothes and shoes that would make me look more feminine. Since I had never worn high-heeled shoes before, we both agreed that it was safer for me to get shoes with just a one-inch heel. You see, I never wore makeup or a dress that would contour to my body, until Yuon's sister showed me the ropes.

After we finished shopping, we went back to her family's house.

"Boy, I am tired," I uttered.

"Try on the stuff we got," Jahil said.

"Alright! I'll go and get changed."

I went to the bathroom and changed from my sporty clothes to a beautiful dress that gave surprising definition to my body. I opened the bathroom door and stood there, waiting for Jahil to say something.

"Well?"

"You look great. Now try to walk down to the living room."

I walked down to the living room like a block.

"Now try to walk with one foot over the other and let yur hips go out like this."

While I practiced walking with more emphasis on my hips, Yuon came in from his motorcycle ride. My tight skinny dress and heeled shoes grabbed his attention so much that he eventually started to hang out with me again. Later on, I found out that our relationship was not monogamous. He was promiscuous. Despite of this fact, I still had strong feelings for him.

Despite all this chaos going on with my love life, I made it through on my first year of college. I decided to spend my summer at my cousin Yoon's house on Hempstead, Long Island. That way I could still see Yuon and have a place to stay for the summer break.

Yoon was not my cousin by blood but he was my cousin by his mother's generational name relation. Our Foochow culture was somewhat different than the typical Chinese culture. In Foochow culture, we had a book that listed all the surnames and each surname had list of generation names that helped the descending generation to keep track of what line they are in.

A list of characters was given to each proceeding generation. The male usually carried the generation names. A boy might get a name with the first character of the generation name; the second character would be his own name.

Yoon's mother has the same surname as my father, and her brothers carried the same generation name as my father, so they addressed each other as sister and brother. In Foochow, we called this "Onna." Yoon was my cousin by a relation of the same Onna from his mother's side. I asked my Foochow friend if other Chinese had this Onna and she said she didn't know.

I called Yoon my pseudo-relative. It was a weird concept for Americans to grasp, as well for me. He had three children, Iddle, Nilsa and Sandy.

When I was younger, I would spend a few summers there, just to get away from the city and socialize with his daughters who were closer to my age. My cousin owned a Chinese take-out restaurant, and when I came for a visit, his daughters and I would gather around this stainless steel sink and peel the skin off shrimp while we chattered on. We would send "I miss you" cards back and forth to each other when I was away in the city during the school session. We were close friends, although technically they were my nieces. But our relationship began to shift in an unfavorable direction on this summer visit.

Whenever Nilsa, Sandy and I wanted to go out, we would lie to their parents that we were going to the library to study, or we were going home to take a nap. In my Foochow upbringing, if we candidly told them that we want to go out and have fun, they would consider us to be immature and lazy and declare that was all we cared about. Because in their time, when they were our age, they had to work hard all the time to help support the family. I guess they didn't realize that we were living in a different generation than they were.

"You want to meet my boyfriend? We can do something together," I asked Nilsa and Sandy.

"Who is your boyfriend?" Sandy inquired.

"He is someone I met in school."

"Sure, we could do that…" Nilsa suggested.

"Where are we going?" Sandy interjected.

"I was thinking we could go to a bowling alley."

"We have to think up of something to tell my Dad where we're going," Nilsa declared.

Nilsa and Sandy told her parents that we were tired from working in the restaurant, and we wanted to go home and relax. Once we went home, Yuon came over and picked us up in his car.

In the bowling alley, Yuon and I danced to the jukebox music together. We pressed our hips against each other and swayed to the rhythm of the music. "You dance like you were doing it," Nilsa told me later. I was too ashamed to broadcast that information so I remained silent.

I wanted to get a job for my summer break. Yuon worked at a nursing home as a housekeeper, and I was able to get a housekeeping job through my connection with him. I didn't have a driver's license, nor a car, so I had to take two buses to get to work.

The housekeeping uniform requirement for women was pink pants and shirt. I got the uniform the day before my first day of work. The next day, I got up a little earlier than I needed, to get ready for work. I didn't want to miss the buses, and I didn't want to be late on my first day.

I left the house early in the morning, before dawn. I walked at a steady pace to the bus station. But when I realized that someone was following me, I started to walk faster. The person behind sped up as well. I turned around to see who it was, saw a man with an Afro, and before I realized what was happening, he quickly threw hard multiple punches in my face and knocked me out of consciousness.

He went away, and left me there on the ground motionless and helpless. My clothes were covered with blood. I don't know how long I stayed on the ground until a taxi driver passed by me and called the police. The police asked me in my semi-conscious state where I was staying. I gave them the address in my groggy voice.

The ambulance siren sounded as they rushed me to the emergency room.

The police drove by my cousin's house and hammered on his storm door. *Who would be knocking so hard this early morning?* my cousin's father wondered as he opened the inside wooden door.

"You speak English?" the policeman asked.

He shook his head and went upstairs to wake Yoon. Yoon came strolling down the stairs to see what was going on. "This lady was knocked out unconscious," the policeman said, showing him my college picture I.D. "She says she lives here. Are you her family?"

He nodded.

"We rushed her to Mercy Hospital E.R."

My cousin called my Mom and Dad in the city and picked them up to take them to Mercy Hospital. I didn't know how long I was unconscious in the emergency room, but I did remember it was quite a long time. The medical staff did various tests on me: rape test, X-ray and other needed tests.

My left jaw was broken. They did a surgery on my left jaw by realigning the broken pieces of bone with wires. My jaw was wired to the teeth for 6 to 8 weeks. My teeth were held together with small rubber bands; I had a fracture on the bridge of my nose.

I remember lying on the hospital bed unconscious, then seeing a bright light above me and starting to come back to consciousness. I opened my eyes and saw a hospital chaplain sitting by my bedside praying in a dim room.

Once I passed the critical stage, they sent me to an inpatient hospital. I lay on my bed with bruises all over my face. "This wouldn't happen if you were home. Your Dad accidentally pushed over the Buddha the night before. He caused a bad omen. The black guy you go with set this up," Mom rambled on.

"Stop it. Shut up or leave." My mother didn't know about Yuon until this and she didn't approve of us.

She rambled on a little longer before she quit.

When the nurse helped me change into clean hospital clothes, my mother saw my droopy breasts and according to her that was a sign of me losing my purity.

"*Iyol!* You broke your virginity," she said with a heavy sigh.

"Leave! I don't want you here," I screamed at her in my fragile state.

She didn't want to leave because she wanted to take care of me, so she stopped complaining again.

My physical condition got worse, and I was having muscle spasms and trembling. I wasn't taking my medicine while I was in intensive care. The medicine that Bellevue Hospital prescribed me after Tegretol was Quinine. Quinine didn't help me until I found God.

Mom visited me in the hospital as often as she could and when I was released she took care of me and nursed me back to health as best as she knew.

I couldn't eat anything solid for about 2 months while my jaw was wired shut. The bruises on my face faded away in the next few weeks.

When they removed the wire from my mouth, I had an altered sense of taste. I was anxious to eat something solid after being on a liquid diet for months. The first thing I had was egg drop soup and it tasted plain and hard as a rock. It took me a while to get my normal sense of taste back.

I could only open my mouth a little bit. It took me years to get my mouth to open the way it should.

After my recovery, the medical bills began to pile up. I applied for Medicaid but unfortunately I was denied. I filed for an appeal. During my hearing I stated that I was a victim of assault, and it wasn't my fault that I accrued these expenses. After the hearing, I stopped getting bills from the hospital and doctors.

I lost a lot of weight during that time and I had to take a semester off, even though I didn't want to. I wanted to be on schedule for my graduation. My focus was to get my bachelor's degree in four years but I had to take care of myself first.

After I got better, I called Nilsa and Sandy to see how they were doing, but their response was distant. I sent them "I miss you" cards but they didn't send any back. Eventually I stopped trying and our relationship dissipated.

Stony Brook

M y mother wanted me to apply to schools that were close to home. She convinced me that I would be safer, and she would look after me.

Yuon's sister went to one of the CUNY (City University of New York) schools called York College. I didn't know what school to apply to, so I asked her about her school. She thought it was a decent school, so I asked her to get me an application. I was still talking and seeing Yuon secretly during the time that I was out of school for a semester. Of course, he was very remorseful about what happened to me.

I got accepted to York College in Queens. I was ready to accept my mother's proposal that I would be safer closer to her, but later I came to my senses and remembered why I went away in the first place.

If bad things were going to happen to me, they could happen to me anywhere. I didn't think going to school in the city would alter it. In all honesty, I was very frightened of being assaulted again, and if I had a nurturing and supportive environment to go to, I would be better able to deal with my fear of being outside again.

Unfortunately, I didn't have that luxury. I needed to be strong, resilient, and push forward. I needed to think for myself and choose what was the best for me, not what my mother thought was best for me. I couldn't let fear dictate what I did and where I went to school.

I went back to Farmingdale in the spring of '91 in faith that I was going to be okay. My mother didn't understand that I was happier when I was away from them. She didn't even know my pain or about my suicide attempts. She thought she could keep me safe, but she couldn't. Her keeping me on a short leash wasn't going to help.

Since I was out a semester, my dormitory arrangement changed. I was in a different building with a different roommate. My roommate told me that she really wanted to room with her best friend and asked me if I could move somewhere else. I found a girl who needed a roommate in the same building so I moved in with her. Later, I discovered that her best friend never moved in with her, and she got the room all to herself. Was she just telling me to move so she could have the room all to herself?

It was stressful coming back to school from a very traumatic experience. My body was so tensed up that it was in a fight-or-flight mode, and I experienced insomnia in the beginning of the semester. My mother had been calling the dormitory's public phone every night to check in on me. Sometimes she got hold of me and other times she didn't. "Cindy, you got a phone call," my hall-mate knocked on my door.

"Thanks."

I answered the phone, and my mother asked me where was I when she called earlier. "I was in the library studying," I said.

"The library is open late at night?" she interrogated.

"Yes!"

"Don't do it."

"What do you mean?"

"Don't do it, you know."

She meant sex. That was my relationship with my mother. Instead of listening and talking to me, she told me what to do and not to do, and she assumed the worse of me. I was so glad that I didn't let her talk me into going to college locally.

One evening I was in the library studying, I felt the stress caving in on me. I went to the restroom and lay on the tile floor and started to sob bitterly and relentlessly. I let out all my emotional anguish about the disappointment of Lydia not going to college with me and everything that had happened to me. I felt a surge of relief after I wept.

Letty and some other people on campus heard from Yuon about what happened to me, and they asked how I was doing, and if I was okay, when they saw me. I told them I was.

I met some new friends from the Asian Association Club, including a girl named Kim. She lived off campus and sometimes she stayed late in my room. Some evenings at night when we got hungry and the cafeteria was closed, we would take her car to White Castle and order burgers.

In the White Castle restaurant, while I waited for our orders, Kim shared something disturbing.

"Cindy, you know Yuon gave me a ride in his car and before he dropped me off, he whipped out his penis and made an indecent proposal."

"Oh, really!" I didn't share with Kim about my history with Yuon. My relationship with him was in limbo. I only saw him if he came to visit my dorm and he just wanted one thing from me: sex. This just made me not want to see him ever again. I had enough of this nonsense from him and I was ready to move on.

"That just turned me off. I told him that he was not going to get it and I walked out."

Back on campus, word got around that the Asian Association Club was planning to have a ballroom dance party. I went to the library to get some studying done, and I saw Tony there at a table reading his book. He was a new friend I met in this term. He was a Latino about 5'5" in height. I went over to his table.

"Hi, Tony. How is it going?" I whispered.

"Hi, Cindy. Hey, are you going to that ballroom dance party?"

"Yeah."

"Well, you want to go together?"

"Sure!"

I wasn't sure if this was a date since there wasn't any arrangement of him picking me up. On the day of the event, he told me that he would meet me at the place, so I guess this wasn't a date. It was just a friendly gathering.

I saw Tony at the dance and he approached me. "Hey, you look pretty today," he said.

I had my white rayon classic skirt suit on, and had sprayed and gelled my hair and put on make-up.

"Thank you, Tony."

The room was filled with noises of people yakking, and music playing in the background. Friends that I had met through the Club were there. Kim had a black dress on and Tieh wore a suit and tie. There were a lot of people from different schools at the event.

I looked across the room, and I saw a cute guy sitting at one of the tables. "Who is that guy sitting over there?" I asked one of my friends.

"I don't know."

I went over and introduced myself to him.

"Hi, my name is Cindy. Are you from Farmingdale?" I asked.

"No! I am from Stony Brook."

"Oh, really. What is your name?"

"Raymond."

"How is it over there?"

"It is good. I think it is a good school. I could show you around when you visit."

"That would be nice. I am thinking about changing schools. Stony Brook sounds okay."

"You want to dance?"

"Sure!"

I didn't know how to dance ballroom, so I just followed his lead on the dance floor. In the end Raymond gave me his number, so I could call him whenever I wanted him to give me a tour of the Stony Brook campus.

I called Raymond a couple of times, and I found out that he didn't have any romantic interest in me. It was just a friendly gesture of him to offer to give me a tour around the school. That was too bad because he was cute and nice.

I got involved with another guy on campus who was no better than Yuon. I just wanted somebody to get my mind off Yuon. I was on a rebound from one bad relationship to another.

I wanted to get out of this environment and start a clean slate. One day I said to my sociology professor that I would like to study in the field of sociology. I was interested in going to

Stony Brook but I was afraid that I might not have the grades to go there.

"Come, follow me to my office," the professor said.

When we got to her office, she called the Stony Brook admission office, and spoke with one of the admission counselors of my interested going to Stony Brook, and how I was afraid that I might not get the grade I needed to transfer over.

"To transfer over she would need an 2.5 GPA," the admission counselor said

"She is really a hard working student and I think she would be an asset to your university. Otherwise I wouldn't make this phone call for her, "my professor stated.

"Tell her to go ahead to make the transfer and if she doesn't have the grade that is needed, tell her to give me a call. We can work something out."

My sociology professor told me that majoring in sociology can open doors to various job opportunities. I got the transfer application, put my choice of major as sociology, filled out all the necessary information and sent it out.

I was really having a hard time with my biology class, and I was afraid that I might not get the grade I needed to transfer, even thought the admission counselor told me that I could call her and something could be worked out. If I got the grade I needed, it would be a sure thing that I'd be transferring to Stony Brook. I wanted a sure deal, not uncertainty, and I didn't know what would be that "something" that they could work out. What if that something couldn't work out? Then I would be stuck in Farmingdale for another semester. I wanted to break the emotional entanglement of these bad relationships I had developed, and I felt I could only do it if I changed the scenery.

I usually had a hard time in the field of science. I didn't really get a good foundation of it during my rudimentary education. Being in Special Ed. classes, I didn't get to learn the stuff that mainstream students got to learn. Certain subjects I had a harder time comprehending without special help and attention.

I wasn't able to get the extra help I needed. I tried really hard to study for the biology final exam, but despite of my effort, I wasn't fully getting it. I desperately wanted to leave this place so I resorted to cheating on one final exam question. It was nothing I was proud of.

On my biology final, I wrote one of the essay questions and the answer on a small piece of paper and kept it in my winter coat pocket. Imperceptibly I took that piece of paper out, and copied the answer on the essay paper. I was so scared and wondered what would be the repercussion if I got caught cheating.

The professor was watching us closely. Once I finished copying, without him suspecting anything, I turned in my paper.

I got the grade I needed at the end of the term to go to Stony Brook University.

Meeting Richard

S tony Brook University was rated top 100 Best National Universities by *U.S. News & World Report* and top 2 percent of universities worldwide by the *London Times Higher Education Supplement* and the Institute for Higher Education in Shanghai. The credentials just went on and on. I didn't know I went to a prestigious university during my enrollment years.

On my registration day, I met another person from Farmingdale who also had transferred to Stony Brook. His name was Dougee. He had cerebral palsy and was in a wheelchair. Later I became Dougee's personal aid and a friend, helping him with cleaning his room and getting dressed in the morning.

The Stony Brook campus was much bigger than Farmingdale, with a 1,100 acre campus, and its Asian student population was much bigger as well. I met numerous friends and some of them were from my high school. Jean, Lynne, Molly and Anne weren't my friends when we were teenagers, but when we bumped into each other on campus and realized that we were from the same high school, we became friends.

My dormitory building was far away from the main campus, and I didn't like the distance I had to walk to all my classes. So eventually I moved to Roth quad, Mount building, which was closer in. On my first day of school I had a full schedule, not finishing class until 9:20 p.m.

I was able to get a part-time work in the sociology department as a data entry clerk. Luckily I got financial aid through a Pell Grant and the College Work Study Program, a federally funded program that assists students with the costs of college.

In the summer of 1992, I decided to take some summer courses, so I could graduate on time. Living in the dorm in the summer cost more money than a regular session, so my friend Jean found a place off campus. We had to walk at least a half-hour from the house to the campus bus station. There was five of us in a-one bedroom duplex: Renee, Amy, Lynne, Jean and me.

Jean and Lynne slept on one big mattress in the bedroom, and I slept on a mattress on the floor at the end of the bed. Renee and Amy slept on another mattress in the living room floor. They hammered nails into the walls at each end of the room, strung a rope on the nails, and hung a big piece of fabric on top of the rope to conceal their mattress. In this way they sort of had their own little room.

One of my classes was Chinese literature in Javit lecture hall. In the class, there was a guy named Richard, who was very handsome, with light brown hair and brown eyes. When we took a class break, we stood outside the hallway and conversed a little.

"Hey, are you from Stony Brook?" I asked.

"No, I am from Columbia University."

"Then what are you doing here?"

"I am just home for the summer break and thought it would be nice to take a course to keep me from being bored."

"Oh really? You get bored from not being in school?" I giggled.

He smiled and laughed as well.

"What is your major?" I inquired.

"Asian Studies."

"So that is why you took this class."

The break was over and it was time to go back to class. At the end of the class, he offered me a ride home so I didn't have to walk so far to my house. While he was driving, he turned his head toward me, and our eyes met for a brief second and we smiled brightly to each other.

"Oh, I don't know," he muttered.

"What don't you know?" I replied.

"I don't know much."

We exchanged phone numbers, and we talked to each other between classes. I had a dream that we were dating and that he went to China to study or work abroad, and I was very upset and missed him very much.

I woke from the dream feeling weird about it. I told him only part of the dream, the part that he went to China.

"That is weird. I was thinking about going to China," he said.

As time progressed, he took me out on a date. Not knowing the proper etiquette, I wore a sleeveless dress on our first date but neglected to shave under my arms. I asked him if I should wear a jacket, and he told me I should.

He was too ashamed to be in public with me with hair under my armpits but he didn't know how to convey this to me. Later as we got to know each other better, he felt comfortable telling me that was bothering him. I shaved my armpit hair for him and for myself.

I had a week off to transition from summer courses to fall semester. Wow, I got a week not using my brain for academic purposes! My boyfriend helped me moved all my belongings from the off-campus duplex to my new dorm using his car.

When we went to check in, the residential staff told me that my spot was taken and they had assigned me to Wagner building. I didn't want to live so far away from the main campus so I went to residential office to see if they something nearby. Luckily, they were able to find me something close by.

We drove to Roth Quad, Mount Building to check in, and got my keys to the front door and my room. Rich helped me to transport my belongings from his car to my room. When he was done, he lay on the sheetless mattress to take a break. I lay beside him. He turned around, and gave me a kiss, and told me he loved me. This came as such a shock to me that I wasn't able to say the same back to him, but I had a big smile on my face.

We went out for dinner, and while we were waiting for our meal to be served, my mind wandered to what I need to do tomorrow.

"Where is the food? How come they are not here yet."

"Easy! After dinner I will drive you back then you can organize your schedule for tomorrow, "he replied.

I felt comforted and at ease.

On the third week of school, Molly and her boyfriend Brian invited a group of people to play softball in Central Park. I went back to the city on the weekend to see Rich and decided to join the game.

I was not familiar with the rules, so Brian taught me how it worked. I practiced catching the ball with Brian, but he inadvertently threw the ball at my nose and it bled. I had to stop playing and sit on the bench.

"This is great. First time at the game and I got a nose-bleed," I muttered under my breath. "Hey Brian, I am going to sue you after college," I hollered across the field. Brian smiled and chuckled.

Every five minutes, he would come over to check on me, and I told him I was alright. My boyfriend came later and I briefed him on what had happened. He got concerned about my nose. "Are you O.K.?" he kept asking.

After the game, we went out for lunch. It was a pretty big group, about thirteen of us. When lunch was over the group split up, and some of them decided to go to the Metropolitan Museum. We went along with that group.

We saw a lot of ancient monuments. I was especially eager to see the Chinese garden, but I was disappointed when we found it. It wasn't as spectacular as I had expected. It was just a small indoor garden.

I thought Rich was a great guy. He was gentle, sensitive, caring, and loving. He paid attention to everything I said. I considered telling my Mom about him but I wanted to see where she stood in regard to a white guy.

Back in my parents' apartment, I ventured, "Aren't white people nice?"

"No, they are no good," she answered.

Well, I guess I won't be telling her about Rich. *Why can't she accept the person, not the race?*

Rich and I dated for approximately two years, not counting the time when he was overseas in China. My dream about him going to China, and me getting disappointed, came true.

It was a long distance relationship when we were in school, and some weekend when things got busy with school work, we wouldn't be able to see each other for as long as two weeks.

I graduated from Stony Brook in our first year together, and he graduated from Columbia in our second year. Then he went to China for two semesters teaching English. While he was gone, I felt lonely and depressed, and missed him tremendously.

I was living at home without a full-time job. I wanted Rich to rescue me out of my misery and I wrote him a letter telling him how miserable I was living at home and how much I missed him.

He missed me during his first few weeks away, but when things got going with his job, he stopped missing me, and had a change of heart about me after he received my letter. He was my first love. He broke off with me over the phone when he came back to town. He didn't have the courage to do it in person.

I was devastated by this breakup. I loved him dearly, and he was the only guy at the time that had treated me with respect, kindness, and gentleness.

I wished I didn't cry on his shoulder with my letter about how miserable I was living at home. Things might have been different, and I might be on a different path of life, but in any case I was glad it ended. I was leaning on him for my happiness and security, and wanting him to rescue me.

I didn't think any relationship should continue with this as its foundation.

My Diagnosis

In February 1995, I was at last properly diagnosed, but it took years after that to be connected with the right medical professional to help me to get the help I needed and to have a better understanding of it.

A neurologist at Stony Brook University Hospital, Dr. Rosen, prescribed me Baclofen and told me to discontinue Quinine. When Baclofen wasn't working, and I was suffering out of control twitching and trembling, he told me to go back to Quinine, but that didn't help either. I called the doctor every day as my condition worsened. He didn't seem to care or know what else to do for me, except to tell me to give Baclofen time to work in my body.

I couldn't stay still to rest my body to get some sleep, nor could I do anything else. I was lying on the bottom of the bunk bed all night until the next morning, trembling out of control. Finally I decided to call 911 to go to a nearby hospital.

Before the ambulance came, I called Brian to find out which hospital had quality care and was reputable. He informed me either Cornell Medical Center or NYU. I called Darin, another friend, to come and give me moral support in the emergency room.

Darin was a friend from Stony Brook University. We lived in the same dormitory building, but on different floors and rooms. Our friendship was purely platonic.

The paramedic came up to the second floor of my parents' apartment with an ambulance bed. They asked me about my medical history, and which hospital I wanted to go. I told them Cornell Medical Center.

They strapped me to an ambulance bed, and were about to carry me down the stairs to the ambulance, but my mother stood in front of the bed, and asked where I was going to be. I asked the paramedic the address of the hospital and gave it to her.

I specifically told her that there was no point in her going there, because there was nothing she could do to help, given the fact she didn't speak English and didn't how things worked. I didn't want to hurt her feelings, so I told her she can come if she wanted to. That was a big mistake on my part.

In the hospital emergency room, they put me in this little private area, where they were evaluating and filming my movement disorder. My mother found the hospital and came to my room. She didn't know what was going on, so she asked a lot of questions.

With the condition I was in, it was better for her to be quiet, and just be there as a moral support, but she didn't do that, even thought I had asked her not to ask a lot of questions.

I forewarned her about who will be coming. "Mom, my male friend will be coming to help me out and he is strictly a friend."

"Well, as long as you don't give him what he wanted."

It was stressful to be with her and listen to her insinuations. She didn't trust anything I said or trust me, period. She was causing more trouble than she was helping. *I wished she would leave and let me work this out.*

The nurse came in to ask me some questions. Mom asked if the nurse got the right patient. When my friend Darin finally showed up, her face contorted, because he was black.

The nurse told me that only one person could stay in the E.R. and I chose Darin over my mother, and I told my her to go home, and if I was hospitalized I would have a Foochow friend to give her a call.

"Who is this friend that is going to call me?" she asked.

My face cringed and I was aggravated with her badgering questions, and I trembled more. I wished she would be a good sport, and just take what I said without feeling a need to know all the details.

The nurse intervened and said this was enough; she needed to get some rest, so my mother left. I got the best quality care in the E.R. The nurse brought me food, and I was well taken care of. The doctor and nurse were very attentive to my needs.

They gave me Artane, and it was able to control the muscle spasm immediately. I was diagnosed with Dopa-Responsive Dystonia. They prescribed me Sinemet, as a regular medicine regimen.

I felt great taking Sinemet. I was able to do anything that I wanted, but the negative side effects— confusion, agitation, anxiety, insomnia, and stiff muscles—were taking a toll on my personal life. I switched from pharmaceutical medicine to nutraceutical medicine, so I didn't have to deal with any of the negative side effects, with the help of the Dr. Joel Robbins clinic in Tulsa, Oklahoma.

Cindy Yee Kong

I moved to Tulsa, Oklahoma in 1999 from New York, and years after that, things started to come together in regard to being educated about my disease and getting proper help.

I went to see a speech therapist around 2008, regarding my communication problem. I was getting frustrated with people having a preconceived notion of me when they heard my accent. They immediately assumed I was fluent in Chinese, and English was my second language, and that was why I had a hard time understanding certain things.

My initial reason for going to see a speech pathologist was to eliminate my accent, but as I discussed my problem further, I found out that I had a bigger problem than I thought. The Speech-Language Pathologist, Janelle Connor, evaluated me and took note of my medical diagnosis.

"I don't understand why I have problems in both languages. Shouldn't I at least have grasped one of them? I have problem understanding certain things in both English and Chinese, and I speak with an accent in both," I vocalized my defeat to her.

In her evaluation, she wrote:

> Yee Kong has been in my care for several months for speech and language difficulties. These difficulties include articulation or speaking clearly; social language, i.e. poor eye contact and limited facial expressions; and auditory processing difficulties, discriminating between words and sounds and voice inflection.
>
> She may experience trouble in producing clear speech, expressing feelings through facial expression, and comprehending complex phrases. Yee's best form of learning will be

through kinesthetic or visual means; directions should be given through written means as a supplement to auditory directions.

She has difficulty remembering items given auditorially and required additionally time to process information given orally or in a written text. All her oral structures, which were secondary to Dystonia, were weak. She required spoken words repeated or in a written text.

She appeared to have significant difficulty communicating with other individuals resulting from flat affect, poor social skills, poor articulation skills, limited auditory processing skills and general use of the English language. She had reported that people often thought she was mad due to her lack of facial affect.

In addition, she stated that people often didn't understand her. She sought out speech therapy due to ongoing difficulties communicating with others.

Because of her medical diagnosis of Dopa-Responsive Dystonia, which responds much like Parkinson's disease, she may require several small breaks throughout the day. As she becomes more fatigued or stressed, you can expect to see a decrease in overall motor function, facial expressions, slurred speech and less understanding through auditory means.

When I was in school, I learned to compensate for my deficiencies by getting copies of notes from other students in class. I would ask the professors to let me take the test a half-hour before class or stay after class to finish it.

From Janelle Connor, I was able to make a connection with another speech pathologist name Tamille Cookery, who introduced me to Cognitive Rehabilitative Therapy, founded by Dr. John Hatfield.

Throughout my life I have problems focusing from one task to the next. I would go about doing what I needed to do and when I moved from one task to the next, I would forget what I was supposed to do next. I would stare at the blank space for a few minutes, trying to remember what I was supposed to do next.

I also had problems with visual scanning and registered what I saw quickly. If I were in a reading group or a class, and I had to locate a certain text to catch up with the group, or if I needed to find an item in a store, my eyes would just stare straight into the space.

I thought this kind of problem was just normal until I went through the cognitive therapy. The therapy helped me to realize that I had a bigger problem than just these I mentioned above.

It helped me to focus on my task without getting lost in the midst of it. I was able to scan through material to catch up with what someone was reading, and search for things in the grocery store or at home.

In addition, I had more clarity in my speech and I was able to grasp some auditory information to a point if the person slowed down their speech pattern. I have more focus, problem-solving and critical thinking skills than before, and better memorization. I am able to hold a thought in my head and manipulate it quicker. I can add and subtract in my head without having to write it down on paper.

It took me a year to finish the whole program. Then I went to Oklahoma State University's speech clinic for further therapy. This intern clinician, Alice, assigned me oral motor exercises to maintain speech articulation.

In the fall of 2011, this intern clinician was adamant that I do the oral motor exercises daily and she followed through in our session together. This eventually helped me to build some muscles in my face which helped with the droopy look. She also helped me with my social skills and in other areas.

In 2012, I went to see a geneticist, Dr. Kruger. I informed him of my diagnosis from my speech pathologist, Auditory Processing Disorder. He said since I had a disease in the brain, it affected my cognitive ability and it shouldn't be separately diagnosed. He did genetic testing on me to make sure that I indeed have Dopa-Responsive Dystonia and to determine whether I carry a dominant gene or not.

The genetic testing revealed that I got two recessive genes, each from both parents. My parents' children had a 25 percent chance of getting it. I was the unfortunate one. It was a gene mutation on one of the genes called Tyrosine Hydroxylase (TH). TH is an enzyme and a gene that is responsible for the production of catecholamine.

Catecholamine is a neurotransmitter that carries one nerve signal to another. It builds a bridge for the signal to go to the next nerve. Essentially my brain was missing a chemical that was essential for human functioning.

Knowing God

I was finally able to get a full-time job as a case manager with the Citizen Advice Bureau in the Bronx. It took me almost a year to get it and move out of my parents' house. Before that, I worked part-time as a telephone ticket agent at Ticketmaster.

I rented a room in a basement in Elmhurst, Queens. There were two rooms in the basement. One was my room and the other was rented by another lady and we shared kitchen and bathroom together.

When weekend came and I didn't have to go to work, I lay in bed lethargically with tears streaming down my face, wondering how was I going to get through the day. I had no places to go to, and no one called me to ask me to go places with them. I would hear this little voice telling me, why didn't you kill yourself. No one wants you here. I would tell that little voice that I didn't know why I was still here, but God wanted me here for a reason.

One day I bumped into an old friend from Stony Brook University, Bob, in the Queens area. He introduced me to the Amway Marketing business and invited me to a business meeting. At the meeting, all I remembered hearing was gaining financial security and the ability to make all this money such that you could quit your day job, so I signed up to be an Amway distributor.

I went to a business convention and shared my estranged relationship that I had with my brothers with one of the ladies there. She told me to focus on my business, and once my brothers see my financial success, they will come around. "Money changes people," she said.

If this lady at the convention was right about how money changed people's attitude, I thought, then if I became successful in the business then I would gain approval and acceptance from my brothers.

The company suggested going to church to get God to bless your business. Of-course, I want God to bless my business. I desperately wanted success so my brothers would pay attention to me. I met a lady named Victoria in the business and she invited me to her church. When I went to her church, I felt the spirit of God tugging on me and telling me that everything I had been searching for was in him. When the pastor asked if there was anybody needed to know God's love, I came up to the front of the altar weeping.

I was looking for love and acceptance in other people. I realized that wasn't the answer to my problem. I wanted to be loved and to know that I am loved. I wanted to find the love that God had for me.

I quitted the business and spent time learning about God's love by reading the Bible, going to church, and going to a Bible study program that the church offered. I learned about God's infinitive love for me and felt his love and acceptance toward me.

I wanted to share his love with my nieces and nephews and the rest of the family. I wrote a letter to my brothers and had a friend translate it into Chinese. In my letter I explained my pain and my journey of coming to know God. I asked them why they treated me the way they did. Unfortunately they never responded to my letter and when I saw them there wasn't any mention of it.

I forgave the wrong that my brothers did to me, and I wanted to show kindness and love to their kids. I didn't want to hold what my brothers did to me against their kids. By showing kindness and love to my nieces and nephews, it was my way of showing my love for my brothers.

Forrest had two children, Millie and Drew, and Bo had two children as well, Myra and Hank. They both eventually were able to own a business and worked for themselves.

Before Bo found a decent business to own and run, he faced financial hardship after he quitted his job. His wife took a job as a seamstress in a factory to help out.

The children were left home alone on the weekend while my brother was out searching for a restaurant, and his wife was working in the factory. When he was home, sometimes the children would get into a typical sibling rivalry, and my brother would get frustrated and smack them.

I visited the kids on the weekend to take them out to the park and did different things with them. I traveled from Queens to Manhattan's Chinatown to show those kids that I care and I wanted to be there for them, when no one was there for me. Some of the memorable events I was able to share with them were Myra's school dance performance that was held in Central Park and the Radio City Music Hall Christmas show.

One visit Myra asked me, "Aunty, the school is having a parent-teacher conference. You want to come?"

"Sure."

I went to their parent-teacher conference and I spoke harshly against their parents for not being involved in their kids' school work.

"They are probably busy with their work," one teacher said, trying to speak kind words about their parents.

I grimaced and said nothing.

I wanted somebody to pat me on my back for being such a great aunt to those kids. I wanted to be recognized for my good deeds, but instead I got opposition from my brother and his wife. My motive was wrong, if I was doing it just to be recognized, but at the same time it was only natural to want to receive praise for some of my good work.

My real motive for doing what I did for those kids was not my own self-promotion but more to be there for them, and to show them that I care.

I regretted that I spoke unfavorably about their parents in front of them. "Don't you ever become like your Dad," I would exclaim to Hank when I was helping him with his homework.

Looking back, I wished I had done things differently. I shouldn't have talked bad about their parents regardless how they failed in their role. I was a bit overzealous in my role to be there for those kids and I might have overdone it. Maybe I was still a bit resentful about my brother even though I thought I was over it. Seeing Myra and Hank get treated the way I had been just brought back some bad memories.

When Myra asked me to attend the parent-teacher conference, I should have asked her to ask her parents first and if her parents didn't want to go, then I would ask them permission for me to go. Instead I assumed that the parents weren't interested and took over their role.

Myra was interested in enrolling in a beginner ballet class. I took the liberty to enroll her and pay for her class without her parents' knowledge. I was interfering with their parental role and I was out of line.

I took them to church and told them about God's saving grace message. Hank accepted the message and I think Myra eventually did too. I will never regret doing that.

I should have worked with my brother and his wife, and encouraged them to get more involved in their kids' lives instead of criticizing them in front of their kids. I was young and foolish back then. Heck, I didn't have a much of a good example to follow.

During that time, their parents didn't like the fact that I was so involved in their children's lives. All I ever wanted was to see those kids excel academically and have a bright future. I tutored Hank with his school work and encouraged him that he was smart and that he could do this.

When Bo found a restaurant in New Jersey, he immediately moved little Hank away, without giving him or me a chance to say good-bye. I was informed by my parents after Hank was gone. I was surprised and shocked that Bo just took Hank away.

Myra stayed at my parents' apartment to finish off her remaining semester in junior high before she reunited with her brother and parents in New Jersey.

"Myra, what is your new address?" I asked.

"My Dad told me not to give you our new address."

I was very hurt to hear that. It felt like a stab in the chest by my brother. Years passed by and I wasn't able to see Hank. I thought about him often and how he used to ask me a lot of questions about why this and why that. *Aunty, why is the moon round? What is the name of that bridge? What is that over there? Why do we have to eat?* I was allowed to see him after he had turned into a teenager, but our connection we once had when he was a kid was gone.

Years before when I was still living on the campus of Stony Brook University, and I was taking an extra course in the summer again, so I could graduate on time. Myra visited me during that time for a week, and she didn't want to leave, because she was enjoying her visit with me. She begged me not to send her home.

I was in a very difficult position. I was trying to finish my education and I wasn't capable of looking after her full time. I didn't know what to do. I tried to make it easy for her to go home, so I threw a goodbye party and invited my friends to come and baked her a cake.

After she left, she sent a drawing of her father hitting her and her crying. I wished I could do more, and know what to do, but I just didn't know what to do. Getting my degree was the utmost priority for me during that period.

Finally I went to her school counselor, and explained the situation to her. I was told by her that she would follow up with Myra. I assumed that Myra's situation was taken care of so I continued in my studies.

After I graduated from Stony Brook University, I followed up with Myra to see if anybody talked to her in school. She said no one ever did. I didn't know if she felt I was abandoning her. I did the best I could, to be there for her.

As time went on Myra moved to New Jersey after she graduated from junior high in New York City. She excelled academically and got a Master's degree in psychology and became a therapist. She got married and had a child. We haven't talked to each other for over ten years. I called her but she didn't return any of my phone calls, so I stopped calling.

Before her wedding date, she emailed me to ask for my mailing address, so she could send me an invitation. I got a bit emotional about the fact that she hasn't called all those years and all of the sudden I got an impersonal email from her. The last time I saw her was at my father's funeral and we exchanged our updated phone numbers and she said she would call me.

I asked her if she had called me in the email. She told me how busy she got with planning the wedding, and said she would call when she finds the time. I felt the treatment I got from my brother trickle down to my niece. I sat in front of my computer bawling in tears and I responded out of my pain: You are just like your father. Never have time for his sis. I typed my email and sent it.

She didn't like being compared to her father, so she fired back with an angry tone in. Things started to get out of hand in our email communication, so I decided to put a stop to it by asking her forgiveness and making peace, accepting things as they were. Email communication is so impersonal that things get misinterpreted and misread.

Not having the right tone or inflection because of my disability affected my relationship with others and my family. My niece Myra stated in her email that whenever I called or wrote, there was always a hint of anger. Honest to God, I wasn't angry, but I wasn't going to justify myself to someone who wasn't willing to call and iron things out on a more personal level.

When Myra was still living at her parents' home, I would visit her and Hank and my other niece and nephew, Millie and Drew, once a year after I had moved to Tulsa, Oklahoma during my single years.

Given the fact that Forrest lived in Maryland, Bo lived in New Jersey, and my parents lived in New York, I would have to visit all three states in one trip. I would visit my parents first, then take a charter bus to New Jersey and after that another charter bus to Washington D.C. to have Forrest pick me up. Forrest lived in Huntington, Maryland, and it was closer to D.C. than Maine. Then I would fly back from D.C. to Tulsa.

The trip was long and tiresome, but I didn't mind seeing my nieces and nephews. It frustrated me when Millie and Drew would always ask their mother's permission whenever I want to take them out for fun. The mother would almost always say no to the request. I remember only one time that she let Millie go with me.

There was a guy named Mike who was a friend of the family and he would come to the house anytime he wanted to and take the kids out for a ride in his car or just to get some ice cream or whatever recreational activities he want to do with the kids. The children didn't call their mother for permission every time he showed up.

I only came once a year and I spent money on airfare and bus rides and endured an exhausting trip to visit the kids. I felt like they didn't trust me. To me that was another form of rejection, saying I wasn't good enough or trustworthy enough to take my niece and nephew out.

The relationship only continues if I initiate contact; when I cease contact, it dies down. What could I expect from those kids? They only do what was modeled to them.

Epilogue

Today I am married to a man that I love for almost ten years. During that period of my marriage, I learned that I have a lot unhealthy behavior or "dry" alcoholism, as some professionals would call it. I might not have picked up a drink but I sure have picked up the behavior. I was controlling, demanding, critical and codependent just like my father, and these behaviors were hurting my marriage, so I sought professional help.

I had seen different therapists throughout the years and was finally able to find someone who was understanding and helpful. I worked out my emotional baggage with my therapist and went to the Al-Anon program. In the process, I learned new healthy behaviors to replace the old sick ones.

I learned in my recovery to be content with what I have and not expect others to fulfill my needs. I learned to trust in God and know that he loves and cares for me. I allowed myself to go through the healing process and cried when I needed to.

I learned to let go of the things that I have no control over. As the Serenity Prayer I learned in my Al-Anon group says, "God, grant me the serenity to accept the things I cannot change, courage to change the things I can, and wisdom to know the difference."

I could not change how others treated me but I could change how I would react to it. I could change my overall outlook on things. Let it begin with me.

When I felt that someone did something hurtful to me, I worked out my emotions by talking to my therapist, writing it down in my journal, or talking it out in my group. After I worked through things this way, I saw them in a different light.

I tend to see everything through the filter of my family, which is not usually a positive thing. That's why I stay away from telling my friends how I feel in the moment. Sometimes it's better to leave things unsaid than say things on impulse that I might regret later. I think generally people like someone who isn't so needy and demanding. I am continually working on placing my trust in God, not in people. Just because I feel something about someone doesn't mean it is accurate. I attempt to find happiness in myself and in God.

I always wanted to be a writer. When I was in college I remember walking from my dorm to class one day, and a thought just passed through my head that I would like to write a book someday.

It was hard for me to keep a job with my disability. I was going from one job to another, not knowing why I wasn't successful in my career. The last job I had was working for the State of Oklahoma as a case manager. I was eventually let go due to my disability. They weren't willing to make an adequate accommodation for me.

It was a blessing, to say the least, to be discharged from that job; otherwise I wouldn't be able to accomplish my dream of being a writer.

My message to you is to never give up your hopes or dreams regardless of where you came from and what kind of upbringing you had. Every challenge in life is an opportunity to do better. If you are not getting the grades you should get in school, then get tested and get help. Nobody is stupid except those with unfulfilled and unreached potential. If you work hard, figure out your weaknesses and do extra to overcome them, then your dream is attainable.

You are your own destiny maker. Don't let where you came from dictate your future. You can rise above it. And know that there is a God that loves you and cares about you.